DID GOD TELL YOU TO GET *MARRIED?*

To:

_____

From:

_____

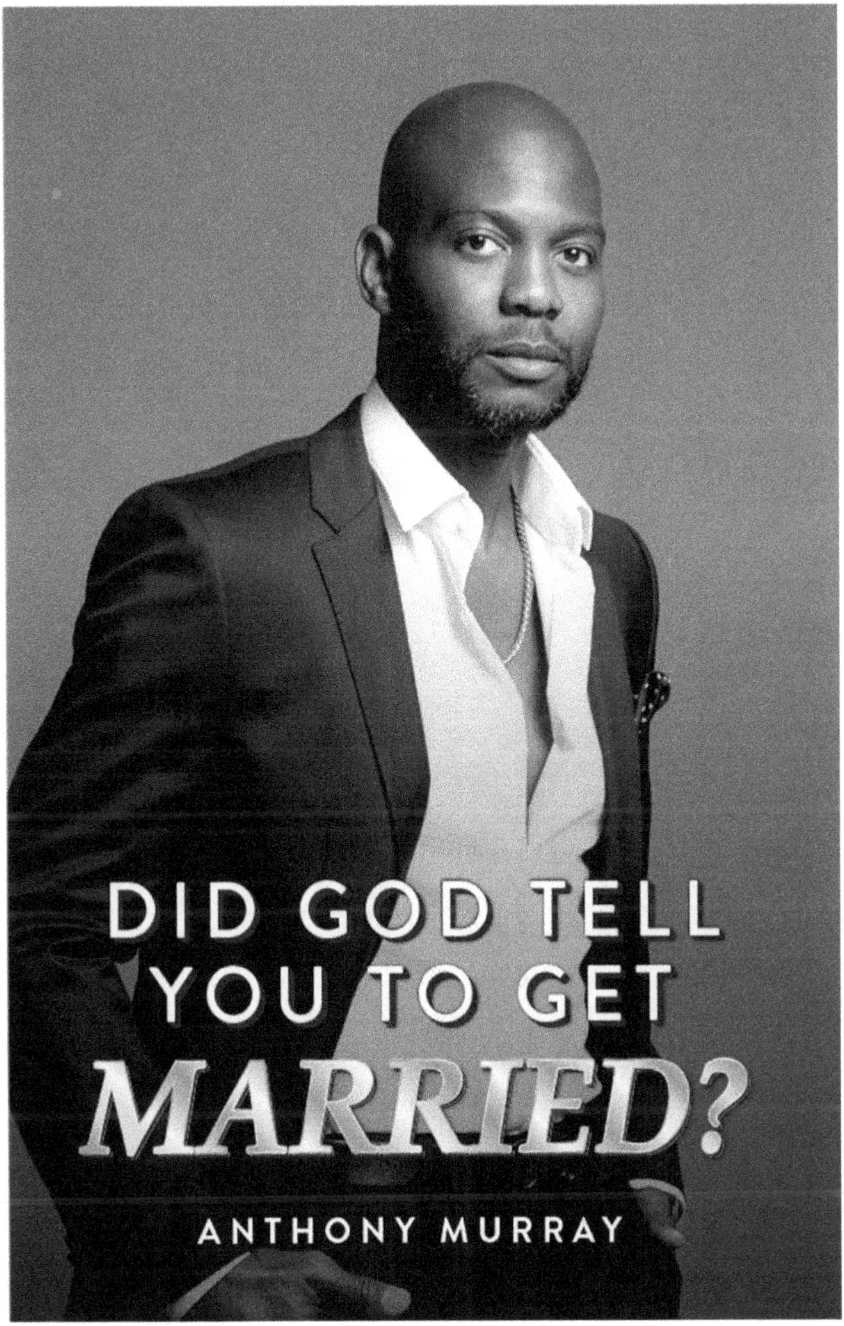
DID GOD TELL
YOU TO GET
MARRIED?
ANTHONY MURRAY

Contents

Introduction

The question has to be answered: **Did God tell you to get married?**

You may hear all kinds of reasons why people decided to marry, and you will hear all kinds of reasons why people want out. Your reason is or will be your own, but maybe if you knew something else the *real reason* will surface.

This book is relevant and helpful for those singles and married people as well. If you are already married you may be questioning whether God told you to get married. If you are not married, read this book and you will be ahead of the game. There is so much more to finding someone and staying together. Maybe your marriage is missing something, or if you're divorced maybe you're looking to build a greater foundation the next time around.

For singles, there is information that will teach you how to avoid making decisions you will later regret. Then there are some of you contemplating divorce. I can't tell you what to do in that situation, but there are some facts you should consider so you won't be shocked, no matter what you decide. After all of this, you must consider if God tells people to get married, how can marriages fail?

If you're married and just can't seem to wrap your head around it working, continue reading to help you come to a clearer understanding. Maybe you're one of those people asking if God designed this marriage for you. What's funny is that at this point, that doesn't matter. Some people come to a bump in the road yet decide that what happened before the bump and what they see after the bump is worth redeeming what they were considering tossing. One person in a marriage can do a 180-degree turn and shift the entire trajectory of the marriage. Everything does not have to be a deal-breaker. It's personal. You have to decide what you want. You will soon grasp it all and make the right decision.

If you're divorced, there are some difficult places you may have to explore. Finding fault isn't one of them but finding out who you are maybe. A marriage takes two, and so does divorce. Whether one person wants it and the other person does not, it still adds up to making a decision that will affect the two of you. Later in this book, we'll discuss how you can move forward.

Many common things that find their way into relationships are tied together between these covers. My own experience as well as information I've found while interacting with couples living in diverse areas has all culminated here. I intend to give you the tools to win.

> **You can overcome anything if you use your inner strength to fight back**

You can overcome anything if you use your inner strength to fight back. Single when you want to be married, divorced and feeling betrayed, married and wanting to get out, or married and needing a change, all can benefit from applying change where it belongs. This book has a hodgepodge of everything. Get ready for the ride of your life. It's going to get wild, so hold on. You're stronger than you think.

You will find everyone is not equipped to tell you what to do. Stop taking advice from your unmarried friends who wouldn't stay married if their spouses spent too much money on groceries. They do not have a clue, but you started the conversation by asking. The "kitchen counselors" aren't using any proven facts, nor have they the experience to advise you. The biggest problem is that these associates have no vested interest in your destiny. Many are miserable and want company. Your unmarried friends might be able to pray for you and provide you with advice in other areas such as your career, but your marriage should not be one of those areas of advice needed from an unmarried person. Seek advice from other married individuals, particularly ones who have been married much longer than you.

Look for the wisdom that can help you get past the pain. Embrace the truths that can explain why it happened. It won't justify it, but it can transition your marriage into something beautiful, give you peace while you're waiting, and comfort you when it just didn't work out. Transition your mind to embrace all that God has for you. It's not that deep. Practical applications to your life are more the glue to hold you together than a perfect marriage to a king in a great palace.

Sometimes marriages work out, and sometimes they don't. Some people are single and satisfied. Yet others have been married twice and are looking for number three. According to *Psychology Today*, some statistics say that first marriages end in divorce 50% of the time, second marriages 67%, and third marriages 73% of the time. My answer to all those numbers is to learn things that work and the ones that don't. You can always end up on the right side of any statistic. Whichever side is good all depends on your situation.

I'm not going to be super optimistic and pretend all marriages can be saved. Some cannot get past the pain of all the marriage has suffered, and divorce is inevitable. You are not alone in what you feel or what you have experienced. Life does get real.

This book is not just going to discuss if God does, ever will, or ever did tell anyone to get married; it's going to break down what happens in most relationships. This is a book about the ups and downs of love relationships and how they work—the good, the bad, and the stuff some won't talk about around others.

The principles I write about will make your life a whole lot better, whether you're married or single. But, as the old saying goes, the truth sometimes hurts. Some can hear, process it, and live in its reality. Then some perseverate on things they cannot change. That's a flaw that can be changed. You just have to change what you once learned was the truth. Your first truths and what you learned about relationships may not be correct.

As you continue reading have an open mind and decide you'll be open to hearing some things about love relationships you have never heard before.

Let's address this again. Does God tell people to get married? Or you can make it personal: did God tell *you* to get married? No one but you can answer that question, but you can get free with the truth of your proficiency. If nothing else, tell yourself the truth.

This is not a fictional story. This is backstory information for those who need assistance in their love relationships. Married, single, or divorced, everyone needs a little support here and there. Here you go! This book was nearly ten years in the making. My heart is in it. I started married, and then I went through a divorce. Because of that, I'm now better equipped to help you. I'm being very transparent. You can put this book down and pick it back up, flipping to the topic you need to read again. It's just like that. "Textbook" sounds too dry, and this is not. No theories here! In it are godly truths that can get you where you want to be in your relationships. Here's a big word for you; it's not fiction, it's *documentarily* (I guess that's a word!).

Living your life in balance is the key to any good relationship. Be an expert on your part, and wherever you find yourself in a relationship will be secondary to knowing you are giving it your best. Whether you believe God tells people to get married or not will be inconsequential. Winning will be your life, thrills will be periodic nuances, and defeats will be minimal.

> **"**
> **Living your life in balance is the key to any good relationship**

This book is intended to answer the question if God ever tells anyone to get married. Whether you are married, single, or divorced, it's time to set the record straight and be blatant about ways to make a marriage work.

To Be or Not to Be

It wasn't until I became single after being married for the majority of my young life that I knew dating had changed so much. All the picks in the field now concerned themselves about the otherwise hidden qualifications of the people they're meeting. I married at a very young age, so you're looking at a young man with two kids who have had twenty-three years outside the dating scene. Boy, was I surprised at the interview questions I encountered from available women. I was looking for gentle conversation and maybe a few dates and found myself being questioned about my sexual preference. This chapter isn't about complaining, but the realities of dating in the 21st century. If you've been out of the game for a while, I want to give you a heads-up.

One big thing I've studied since being divorced is that "unequally yoked" means more than dating someone outside your religious beliefs. I'm not suggesting you take on the battle of trying to convince an atheist to believe in God just because you want to marry him/her. But what I do want to talk about is the people who marry a person whose dreams don't match and whose lifestyles are at two ends of the spectrum. I'm a pastor and the son of a pastor. I've heard the scripture about being unequally yoked with others who do not believe as you do. That simply means you may be unfairly pressured into forgetting what you believe about God to satisfy your other. This chapter is about a far worse matter than marrying someone who does not believe in the God of the universe or does not practice religion like you.

I know people who married someone who didn't believe like them. This is more than one couple, and most of them are happily married. It seems they discovered a way to make it work while raising kids in a peaceful, God-conscious environment. But then there are the couples who struggle at making a happy home when one person has no real desire to continue on an upward trajectory in life. When you take two steps forward, their ways drag you four steps backward. Your life is in constant turmoil because the two of you are going in two different directions. I won't make a judgment call about marrying outside your faith, but I'll say something about marrying outside of your dreams. You'll be doomed to a life of scarring of your destiny. If you can come together with your person and agree to move forward together worrying about whether or not they believe in God won't hinder your relationship. God will take care of that.

> **A marriage with someone who doesn't want much out of life can be damaging to your heart**

So many people didn't look long and hard enough at character flaws before they got married. Marriage with someone who doesn't want much out of life can be damaging to your heart. And I mean that literally. This isn't a judgment on a person who doesn't want what you want. This is a story about not planning out your life beyond having a luxurious wedding and moving into a nice house. Did the two of you talk about children, life goals, family ties, and vacation planning? What about physical upkeep? This may not sound like much, but when you're heading into your tenth year and find your person isn't dreaming and not supporting your dreams, you're in trouble. Character flaws are more than wearing a holey pair of draws. Some things that aren't real textbook flaws may be a flaw to you.

Here's a real case study that may not sound like much to you, but to the person dealing with it, it's a thorn in the marriage. He has a high-level tech job, and she is a schoolteacher. The problem is she's vying to move up in the educational system and eventually become a principal. He, on the other hand, has no desire to do more than what he's doing. She plans all the vacations, takes care of all the kid's needs, cooks, and cleans, while he watches television and plays video games every minute of his off time. His complacency drives her crazy.

Now, I didn't tell you that story for you to judge either one of these people. This is an example of not planning your life together. The wife isn't mad because he doesn't help with housework; she's frustrated because he has no desire to do much else with his life than make a paycheck and relax. Yes, he works hard and makes good money, but she wants more for her life and wants him to want more for his life.

The above is a picture of unequally yoked. This is an easy one because she could have wanted to be an international opera star and he won't cook a hot dog for himself or his kids. At least they're both dreaming locally. His dream is for the next video game; hers is for the time that a school can hire her as a principal. This is the kind of thing you should take note of before getting married. It's not just in the story he's telling you; it's about what he's done with his life before he met you. Was he a go-getter in school, or maybe the star football player with an eye on a Division I scholarship? That's someone looking to do more than work, come home, and sleep. At least he goes on vacation with her, but does he not have a vision for more than a dull life? These two do not match!

If you're already in a marriage like this, some life coaching could help. You shouldn't just complain; get some reinforcement. As long as you're only complaining, nothing is going to change.

Don't be so anxious to be married that you see a good-looking man and jump at the opportunity. I don't care if he has a good job. If his lack of enthusiasm for life is going to get on your nerves, then you're headed for self-destruction. Just because you're frustrated doesn't mean he's going to change. He may not be depressed; he may just be lazy. Why didn't you know that before saying "I do"?

This kind of unequally yoked is more of a vision-killer than the one who criticizes your religious choices. You can hold hands and conquer the world together while you pray for him and give to people. Your spiritual steps will bless both of you. But, if his dreams only take place while he's sleeping, you're going to have some sleepless nights in unhappiness.

Think about this before getting married. If you're already married and the above scenario is your situation, get some help. He may never change, but you may be able to stomach his lack of movement if you decide it's worth it. Nobody but you has to change to guarantee you win.

So ladies, when you're out there in the dating circuit, make sure you take note of past successes of those you date. If at thirty he's still not on the way to some success, then get you a cup of Starbucks together and don't tell him where you live. Make sure you have all your other questions in order too. What kind of people has he dated in the past, and does he keep company with "anything goes" types? If that's not what you want, then one date is a wrap. Have fun but don't get caught out there making decisions that will negatively affect the rest of your life. There is plenty out there to enjoy; be patient.

Do you want to know how to date in the 21st century? You have to be a boss. Go out with confidence. You must know who you are and what you want. Never settle! Men, you need to be confident in who you are, and this includes constantly looking fresh and clean. Whether anyone likes it or not, human beings look at the outside first. All the other emotional connections come after. If you want a good start, look the part. Women want security. They may have a good, stable job or career, but they're looking for mutual upgrading. Coming in looking and being needy is a recipe for disaster on the dating scene. Looking like your job is sucking the life out of you and you want someone to rescue you is not the 21st century way.

Women, your fresh presentation is just as important. Your hair, nails, and makeup must be tight. Never make the excuse of "I'm just running to the store." He might be in Walmart just like you. After looks, you must know what you want. Desperation cannot play a part. If you make a speedy decision you may later regret it. Desperation in choosing a spouse is a game of Russian roulette. You may shoot for the stars and get blessed, or you may hit a pile of trash. Let your dress speak of your success and your words make you stand out from others. Your confidence will show. Do away with the lies because they'll catch up with you. Be honest about your desires and expect the same from the man you're interested in. If you're not honest with yourself, it will be hard to pick up a lie from others. You will take a lie as the truth and vice versa. First, be honest with yourself. Your presentation should be fresh, from looks to your words.

The above are the first things, but of course, there is more you should know for 21st-century dating. Women must decide they're not going to tolerate the drag-on from the men they're dating. At age twenty-five and older, two years is a long enough courtship to receive a proposal. If you're it, then what's he waiting for? During the engagement, a wedding should be in the works. The next two years should be plenty of time to plan your life together. If you're the hold-out, then you're opening the door for him to move to the next one. Men change their minds too! Don't waste time. The sexual life span is different for men and women. Short of sexual dysfunction, women can have their youth stolen with the inability to get it back. Know the differences and plan accordingly. Proactive is a good word to describe dating in the 21st century.

Ladies, don't tolerate the okey-doke. The worst that can happen is he doesn't want to adhere to your demands. In that case, he may not have been the one anyway. It doesn't take men that long to know "she" is the one. Your demands should be the last thing he has to hear if he knows he's found what he wants. Don't let anything else fool you.

According to some research, men use simple points to know if who he's dating is "the one." The dating goes smoothly from the start. The next thing that happens is what does *not* happen. After months of dating, if the conversation of defining the relationship pops up, that's a sure way to know things are coming to an end. The couple will get along well with each other's friends and family members. There may be more, but him being scared of the marriage not working is not a thought (https://www.artofmanliness.com/articles/how-do-you-know-when-shes-the-one/).

Open and honest talks are a sure sign of a relationship on the right trajectory. You must be able to communicate from the start because it won't get better later on. Someone has to start the conversation. She may be an introvert, but that doesn't mean she can't talk. He may be shy, but there's depth to his train of thought. After the initial connection in the looks department, there must be a meeting of the minds. This only happens in speech, not in the bed. Sexual compatibility does not always equate to being equally yoked. Start the way you expect to continue, sharing enlightening conversations.

These are tried-and-true 21st-century dating guidelines. Most of what's written here aren't new but is just now being put in the forefront. Only you can guarantee what will work. Keep the dating alive even after getting married. Stay true to yourself and expect the same from who you are dating. Your foundation will set the stage for a future on the positive side of lasting relationships. Dating is the beginning of what will be a happy life together.

Souls Mate

"Soulmate" is a term that has been around for ages. People meet and fall in love; they get married and start a family. There were certain things by which they measured the love interest to say this person was a perfect match. Something inside them just told them; they felt like they'd always known the person; they just knew it. As far as I've researched, there are varying answers to where the word originated, yet it's still is thrown around as if it's a guarantee in a relationship.

I decided to take the phrase "soul's mate" on a different journey. A beautiful relationship should unlock the hidden treasures bound in the heart of a person. I am calling this souls mating. If you both are fighting to become one, you'll do all you can to pull the best out of your partner. Not only will you bring your mate closer to you, but you'll be enriched by what's coming out in your direction. "Soulmate" needs a makeover. If you Google the word, you'll find many psychologists don't believe the concept exists. But I can almost guarantee that if you work it the way I'll discuss here, you'll never again say someone is your soulmate, but you'll constantly be looking for ways to make sure your souls are mating.

Mating season for animals is studied in most areas of the Wild Kingdom. If you've ever heard cats in heat, you know they sound like babies crying. Cats notoriously make this same sound for other reasons, but male cats smelling the scent of female cats in heat will cry out more than usual, letting her know he's available (https://pets.thenest.com/male-cats-make-sounds-female-cat-heat-7148.htm). They get together, and the rest is history. Cats do not have a soul, but they definitely mate, and quite regularly. I am not just referring to the sexual relationship in humans, but a way to generate the action of souls mating and staying together. Humans' mating season is every day. I guess we cornered the market of the Wild Kingdom.

I own a hybrid car. When I was in the office to sign the purchase papers, I had to sit and hear things about the car I had no interest in hearing. This is the problem right here. Don't you think the manufacturer went through all the trouble to make this car stand out from the rest? I've had it for a while now and have yet to plug it in. The salesman told me it runs much better when it's regularly plugged in. With all my running across town, I can ride in the HOV (high occupancy vehicle) lane simply by the privilege of owning a hybrid vehicle, but I haven't registered my car and received the sticker that allows me this advantage.

Can you imagine how great it would be if your mate was fully engaged with the desires of your heart? Just like I neglected to take advantage of the full benefits of my hybrid car, God does not create something just to exhaust energy. He expects a return on His investment. A good mate will seek to increase everything his mate has to offer. What kind of person would constantly berate the activities of their mate? Why wouldn't you want to benefit from the fulfillment of your spouse's purpose? Anyone not realizing the benefit of a soul living fully contented is a person who thrives on the misery of others. They have not understood the inner workings of God. Tapping into a mate's desires and working to help them manifest is the best thing a spouse can do to help a soul to mate.

Now, you're probably asking how to mate your soul with someone else. The first step is the most profound and will be the foundation of everything that follows. You have to know you're both compatible with your individual purposes. You must be ready to pull out everything that goes along with that purpose. If you're a person who only wants to work and cuddle the rest of the time, it won't make sense to marry an international entertainer. You're not going to be happy from the start. The entertainer won't be fulfilled not being in front of an audience. If you're administrative, this can be a great asset to an entertainer who has little time for keeping their life in order. This is the beginning of mating a soul.

The unhappy people will rest on a level that's not even half the distance of God's design. You know these people by the shortage of joy they bring to others. Their conversation may regularly contain hurtful words about others or the negatives of their home life. People striving to live in the company of mated souls will be constantly on the grind to pull out desires, create roads to fulfillment, and live with the enjoyment of seeing them realized.

Mating souls is never a one-way direction. Each participant is doing the same thing because they've discovered what they both want are compatible results. They didn't make their wants match; early in the relationship they purposely looked for ways to mate. His call went out, just like the tomcat, and she was already ready. It's not the story of soulmates, but what happens when souls mate.

Proverbs 18:22 says, "Whoso finds a wife finds a good thing and obtains favor of the LORD." The favor found in a wife is not magical happening because of a marriage. The reception of favor comes from the union itself. It comes from a wife who does her husband well all the days of his life. Favor is the result of godly living shared by both parties. The concept of finding a wife comes from the man looking for a woman who contains the attributes of a wife along with being a woman who will be happy to complement his attributes. She matches him, and he matches her. Favor is something undeserved but is distributed by God because of His love for His people. Who can stop favor from coming from a relationship where two people seek to become one and are orchestrating the meshing of their souls?

Okay, so here I am talking about souls that mate, but you won't have to reinvent the wheel on what the rules are for marriage. The Bible didn't leave out much. I'll end the chapter with a few guidelines based on references from the Bible. The mating of souls is icing on the cake of a solidly founded relationship destined to stay together.

Follow these guidelines and include the new concept for mating souls for an impactful relationship.

- **1 Corinthians 7:2-5** – Have sex regularly and do not cheat your spouse out of this experience except with permission so you can pray.
- **Ephesians 5:22-33** – Wives, defer to your husband's authority in the home because God made a particular order of Himself—the man and then the wife. With this in mind, the man is to love his wife so much that he takes care of her like he takes care of his own body. Men must be conscious of leaving both their mother and father and attaching themselves to the attention of his wife.
- **I Peter 3:1-7** – Wives must be so conscious of their husband's spiritual development that they practice having quiet spirits to help steer their husbands in the right direction. Husbands must also respect their wives and treat them right to ensure that God will hear his prayers.

After all of that, I will close this chapter with this. Fulfilling all these beautiful guidelines and then working on mating, your souls should take a lifetime ensuring the two of you work on staying together. Doing your best to live up to these standards is the best step you can take to longevity and soul mating.

What Does Love Have
To Do With It?

Being raised in the church, I have heard a plethora of marriage announcements: "God told me to marry you." "The Spirit said that you are my soulmate." I'm sure, whether you grew up in church or not, that you have also heard many, and maybe said one yourself. The question is, does this really happen?

Many of you have heard the various high statistics: the 50% to nearly 60% divorce rate of first marriages for the general population, including those who attend church. I know that all couples have not been surveyed. 50% of all marriages in the United States end in divorce.

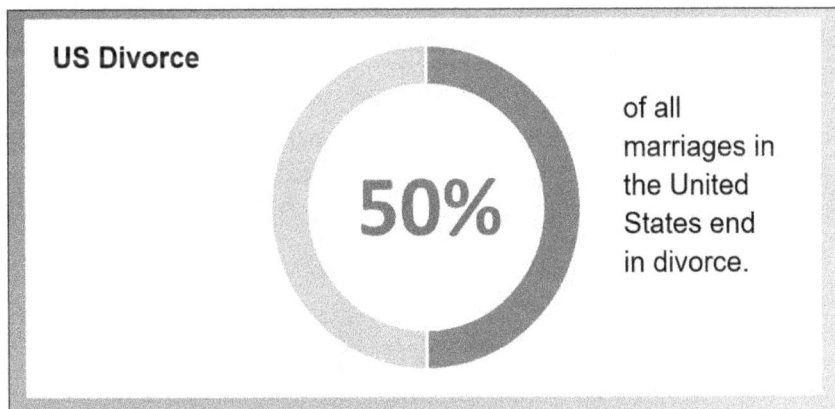

US Divorce

50%

of all marriages in the United States end in divorce.

Out of the 50% who stay married, how many aren't in misery, or how many are just staying for convenience? If you're married you need to get real about the direction of your marriage.

If you're divorced, you may need some new information on dating, and if you're in another marriage it will be smart to find out how much God is involved in your choices.

If you're not married, this book is also for you so you can be ahead of the game and obtain the information for when you are married.

I want to demonstrate practical applications that can teach you how to make changes to enhance and fix your marriage. It's not rocket science and it's not basic math, but if you want to be one working to lower the statistics on divorce, I urge you to understand the principles of dating, courtship, and marriage. What authority are you given in this area of life, and what applications can you employ to use your power correctly?

I know of one instance in the Bible where God told a prophet to marry a prostitute (Hosea 1:2). Maybe this is where some believe God will tell you who to marry. In that story, God was making a point through the life of a prophet, what He was feeling about Israel's constant backsliding. I do not subscribe to the belief. Why would it say that a man who "finds a wife finds a good thing" (Proverbs 18:22)? If God is going to assign a man a wife, then why should the man be looking? On the other hand, I believe some are interested in this question because they're looking for a way out of a bad marriage or can't seem to meet the right man. Either way, both people have some work to do. I'm not guaranteeing any particular result for any particular couple, but the information on love relationships is vast. The only way to correct some errors is to admit that your way hasn't worked.

There are so many more things to discover about relationships that answering this question is of little value. Does God instruct you about every step of your life, whether you should eat spaghetti today or tomorrow, or if you should go to church this morning? I have no idea! Work on the things that can make life better for you. There's so much more to learn.

Let's dive into some questions that might come up when you're married. Is love necessary in a marriage? Now, that's something to contemplate. I say yes and no! The problem is that so many have no clue what love really is. Love isn't infatuation. It's not that fuzzy feeling you get when you meet that person who connects with you physically and you can't wait to see him every day. Anybody saying they always feel in love every day is lying. You can't get along with someone so perfectly that you never fight. You aren't your spouse's clone and everything isn't always agreeable.

A correct definition of love in a marriage is necessary for the union's survival and peace. "Love is an intelligent willingness to surrender self-will, to make sacrifices, to place fidelity, charity, and duty above feelings on behalf of a person . . . " (http://catholicforum.fisheaters.com/index.php?topic=3458512.0;w ap2) Using this definition, you can determine that love is for mature people. Surrendering your self-will is a grand task in and of itself. Then having to add making sacrifices ensures that you have to take your marriage seriously. Sacrificing says you do whatever it is even when you don't want to, and it has nothing to do with feelings. Then you hit that word "fidelity," and I'm sure most of you feel that speed bump in your heart. But if you've decided to tackle this subject honestly, then you're on your way to keeping your marriage out of divorce court.

What you're looking for in marriage is joy, not happiness. Happiness is fleeting. It depends on the happenings. When nothing great is happening and circumstances aren't so perfect, then your happiness will fail you. If your marriage depends on happiness, it will fail pretty quickly. However, there is a place for "happy" in a marriage. That chapter is coming up. I believe this is one of the greatest faults with marriage; people want to always feel in love and want to be continuously happy. Neither is possible. Joy is a continuous flow that comes from two people living together in agreement.

The joy you're looking for in marriage is like a new mother awaiting the arrival of her baby. You've never heard about the happiness of childbirth. When I've been near maternity wards, I've heard everything but happiness. I hear mothers yelling for the needle after the fifth labor pain: "Epidural, epidural, *please!*" This happens as she looks at her partner, thinking of all the ugliest names she can call him, and settles for, "*You did this to me!*" Her poor husband stands there looking pitiful, trying to calm her down. "C'mon, baby, just breathe, breathe; take deep breaths." That sounds nothing like happiness to me! Yet some have enjoyed the process so much they do it over and over again. That's the joy of childbirth. And that's how you must approach marriage.

It doesn't matter how you feel every day. Some days you may wake up and not feel any love for your spouse. That doesn't matter. What does love have to do with it? Go back four paragraphs and you answer the question. The definition that most people use to stay married almost always guarantees a divorce, but the joy of being married is the thing that will keep you in a marriage: fidelity, charity, duty, etc.

Are you marrying a person you can see yourself spending a lifetime with? Or did you go into the relationship saying, "If it doesn't work out, I'll just get out"? I'm serious about this because this approach happens regularly. The word "divorce" is tossed around like it doesn't mean a thing when it's life or death to a relationship where longevity is the goal. You have to look deep at a person before you decide to sign a long-term contract with them. Marriage is supposed to be until death. Although it doesn't always happen like that, it should be entered into with that mindset.

This is not a judgment on those of you who may be in your second or third marriages, or you're divorced preparing for your next marriage. I aim to get you to look at principles that can give your union the foundation to stand under pressure.

This chapter can't answer the question of whether or not God told you to get married. It should make you think about what the real reason was or is. If your answer is some lightweight excuse that's a temporary fix for a present circumstance, then you may want to start digging deep right now for a well-rounded reason. This will be the glue that holds when the storms hit your relationship. If you want to blame God because He told you to marry him, will that make a difference in your heart?

Whether you're currently married, planning your wedding, or thinking about the future, it's never too late to readjust some things. The values you choose to keep you together should be founded on proven facts. How do those couples who have been married for twenty to fifty years do it? What's the glue that holds them together? I suggest you do some research. When you finish reading this book, including referring back to it, ask those you know in long-standing marriages for some keys to staying married. Not only will they confirm some things you've read here, but they'll also give insight that can add to your arsenal.

Only you know the real reason for your decision. But restructuring your foundation can only reinforce any marriage.

Another Look at Soulmates

I've already had a chapter on souls mating, but I want to delve further into this subject because so many don't know how to develop strong, long-lasting relationships. Throughout your life, there's a possibility you can have many soulmates, and I'm not just talking about male and female, husband and wife, boyfriend and girlfriend. There are platonic relationships between soulmates. This is a topic that needs study to help you reconcile yourself in all of your relationships.

There's a story in the Bible about Jonathan and David. David was going to take the throne Jonathan's father, Saul, was currently holding. The sad part of the story is that Saul refused to listen to the direction God gave him for his kingdom and decided to follow his own way. This is why God removed him from the throne. Samuel was the priest at the time, and it was he who gave the leaders the orders that came from heaven. Samuel anointed David as king before the upcoming removal of Saul from the throne. For some strange reason, Jonathan was intrigued by David's escapades in the war although he had never had so much success in battle. This story is found in I Samuel, but the most important verse is stated here: "And it came to pass when he had made an end of speaking unto Saul, that the soul of Jonathan was knit with the soul of David, and Jonathan loved him as his own soul" (I Samuel 18:1).

Soulmates have a lot to do with compassion and admiration for another person. In the above paragraph, Jonathan felt something about David, and he could perceive David's leadership ability. After Saul finished speaking with David something kinetic happened right then in the atmosphere. Jonathan's admiration would soon lead to his active compassion resulting in shielding David from Saul's rage.

This is the climate for soulmates. You may not know why you're connected, but your soul does. I'm going to take a risk now and say something about Jonathan and David. Based on what we know about the relationship between David and Saul, I'm sure Jonathan knew a lot more about his father than David did. After all, Saul raised Jonathan, and Jonathan lived in the kingdom with his father. When he heard the conversation between David and his father, he instantly became attached to David. Every other soldier had been afraid to fight a giant, but not David. Maybe Jonathan was aware of his dad's tender ego. The conversation was not negative, but what David had just accomplished was nothing to scoff at. David would need a Jonathan for what he was about to experience.

David would spend years running from Saul with Jonathan as his backup. Jonathan was his friend the entire time (about fifteen years; II Samuel 5:4).

Since this book is about male-female relationships, I'll relate this heterosexual platonic concept of soulmates to marriage and courtship. You can work to become a soulmate to someone. That little bright light that turns on in unexpected moments when you're building a relationship with someone is where it begins. Maybe you're not even trying to build a relationship when something just happens during a conversation. It's worth researching whatever that is and let it develop; that's what Jonathan did with David. Some people make the relationship a man and woman have in marriage so mysterious, but it can be so much more than having sex and making babies. What if everyone decided they would make someone's soul as close to them as their own? If you can do this, relationships will develop into something unmovable and unshakable, and something unbreakable. No matter where you find yourself with the opposite sex, you can be joined as one human to another with peace as the goal.

Your soul is the seat of your emotions. You didn't make your-

---

"

**Your soul is the seat
of your emotions**

---

self, but your experiences will change the trajectory of how you feel about certain situations in life. Your experiences augment your personality. The way you feel inside is demonstrated by the way you act on the outside. You can make your mouth say anything, but sooner or later what you're feeling in the seat of your soul will be manifested in how you act around and treat other people.

You may not be able to predict how you will turn out ten years from now. You have no control over 100% of what happens to you or around you. Your experiences are directed by where you are, what you've chosen to do, and the people with whom you associate. All of this is part of the development of your personality that starts in what goes on in your soul where your emotions live. Being unable to predict your personality's development is a good thing because just like everyone else you have some rough places, but your experiences can make them smooth. The opposite is also true. Some of your soul's smooth parts need to be roughened up to protect your heart. Don't run from this metamorphosis; embrace it as the life that's designed for you. Yes, you make decisions that affect how you feel, but emotions have tentacles, and your decision does not control all of the reactions around you. You can't tell how someone will respond, and you have little control over what remains in your soul. You'll look up in time and may not be able to figure out how you got to where you are. This is the course of nature taking you to the experiences that form your personality.

Aggressiveness in Conversation

There are many people who want to get married. How that's going to happen is a mystery. You may find this desire written on women's vision boards, in their diaries, or scribbled in notebooks. There's one big problem—getting the information to women that will stop them from blocking their dream. Some conversations turn men off instantly, and some women have no clue what they are. I've heard some women say, "I'm going to be straight upfront with him and tell him what I want, then ask him about himself." This may not work. Getting married isn't that hard, but some tools should be used.

You've heard men are from Mars; women are from Venus. This means the way we think when it comes to male/female intimacy is different. Some people think they can invent their ways and make them work properly. There is a way that could work but it won't be a personal way a woman makes up. None of us is the Creator, but each of us knows what we like. No matter what anyone says, there's a unified way men think about certain things. Women have their ways also, but no matter what you think, times haven't changed that much. Men and women are different. You may as well submit to what works.

For men, it's not always jumping into bed too early that's a complete turn-off. I can all but guarantee it's mostly the conversation. Research has been done that shows women will share every detail of the first date with their girlfriends, but men don't do that.

(GQ Magazine online article: 16 ways men and women date differently, and first date tips for both- Mairead Molloy 2 June 2017.) If the date went awry, a woman will seek out friends to confirm it wasn't her fault. Although most people know men have always been the pursuers, women pursue also. Sometimes this is sexy. But a woman should know the boundaries of her assertiveness. There's a limit to assertiveness and being overly aggressive to the point of turning men off completely.

Did you ever notice most of the things about dating you read talks heavily about what men don't like? You have the age-old warning that men want sex and will try to get some the first day. Some men have multiple women and couldn't care less about the hearts of any of them. Some of this may be true but it's not always the case. Just because a woman lays down in the bed on the first date doesn't guarantee the man won't think she's the one. Don't get me wrong, I'm not advocating one-night stands or exploring sexual relations from the start. What I'm saying is that when men meet the one who comes the closest in their mind of who his wife will be, there's very little she can do to change that. But the one big thing she can do is talk about the wrong stuff.

There has been confusion about the no-nos for women. You've heard what Steve Harvey said in his book about the 90-Day Rule. That may work, but a man may wait ninety days to have sex and still know she's not the one. Then there's the emotional baggage called desperation that can turn a man off instantly. The next big one this chapter is about is trying to get a man to open up on the first or even second date. This is a definite no-no. Men aren't ready for all that emotional mumbo-jumbo when they're talking to someone they don't even know. That's too much vulnerability with someone he may never see again.

Getting to know a woman has more to do with their compatibility than how he feels deeply at the bottom of his heart. You've heard men don't cry. Men can get angry easier but find it hard to tell someone they're hurt. Men have tear ducts just like women, but they're not going to let you see them cry on the first date. As a matter of fact, for some men, you may never see them cry. So asking prying questions about how they were raised by their mother, their absentee father, or the over-demanding siblings may be off-limit subjects along with a bunch of other private things. You can get to know someone without getting every single detail of their private life on the first date.

The art of conversation is really beautiful coming from those who've studied it. By studying I don't mean going to school; I mean knowing how people interact with one another. If you want to get to know a man, then you sit there with your heart open speaking gently and have pleasant conversations. You'll be surprised what you'll find out if you just listen. Fast talking and asking fifty questions from a list and not letting a thought get completed will never yield you the best results. You don't know this man. You're not his counselor. He may not even have a counselor or believe in getting one. He doesn't want to tell you all about his life when you first meet him. And let me say this: it may take years for you to know more about your husband than what you learned before you get married. As you get to know each other, your conversations become more fluid. Circumstances will arise for open dialogue and getting to know each other on a deeper level.

Men will tell women what they want them to know. If women pay close enough attention, they can pick up the signs whether someone likes them or not. It has nothing to do with the sex or how beautiful they are. There are many beautiful women out there suffering along with the ones some may call "unattractive". Men are not dumb. They may be from Mars, but they're an intelligent species. Women and men can know much more than they allow themselves. It's called expansion. I'm suggesting women open up their minds to know how men operate so they can have a better chance of going further with a man than the ones who refuse to change. It may sound like a game, but men know what they want, and they know who to tell their hot secrets to. If a woman hasn't proven to be that special someone, she may not get even a tidbit.

Remember men are looking too. Don't make this search so hard by playing social worker on the first date. You can start a conversation and be as assertive as you like. But don't assert yourself down the wrong road digging into his brain into a sore spot and getting your feelings hurt. Some men are so gentle they won't tell you they won't answer the question. They may not like the fact you're talking about a particular subject, but they know they don't want to be around you and in that atmosphere again. Allow yourself to get to know someone. Men like assertive women, but not ones who will take over their lives and crowd them with their strong minds. They want a strong woman but have no desire to possibly be judged when they tell too much. That's a sign of a woman who may give him hell in marriage. He knows it, and he won't play that game. The men who play that game may even marry you but they're taking a chance. After a while, this kind of man will look for an escape, either by constantly stepping out or spending as little time at home as possible. Don't do it. Be gentle. Talk softly. You'll find you'll get more results by gentle conversations and listening to what he has to say. It's an untruth that men talk less than women. The subject matter is the difference. If you want to go further in a relationship, don't start off grilling him like he's on trial for murder. A man is on the hunt but would rather go hungry than find himself stuck in a relationship with a woman who asked too many hard questions right from the start. Let me give you an example of what questions you should not ask on the first date.

First Date Questions to not ask men

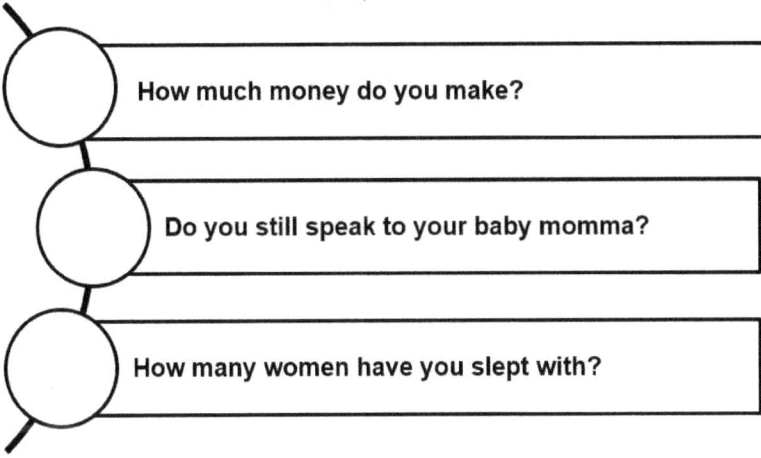

How much money do you make?

Do you still speak to your baby momma?

How many women have you slept with?

Those are very personal. He will share and open up soon enough, be patient. The right time to ask those hard questions would be after you've proven yourself worthy of knowing those answers. What do I mean? Serve him and be attentive to him, then you can ask those hard questions. Let me explain this further. You must treat a person right first. You give and give, then you ask. You earn the right based on how you treat him. That's when you can demand certain things. With a quality person, you can't demand things upfront. A quality person won't allow it. You have to earn it and the person has to earn it, and that's when you ask. It's not about time; it's more so access or a vibe. It can be the same day or three months later. Let me reiterate—it's not about the time.

Asking a man to open up and share the innermost secrets of his heart on the first date is like asking a woman for sex on the first date. Just like you would feel it's too soon, men feel asking too many personal questions upfront is too soon. You may think those two things are on the opposite end of the spectrum, but to a man, it

> **”**
>
> Asking a man to open up and share the innermost secrets of his heart on the first date is like asking a woman for sex on the first date

feels the same way. It's too deep. What you want to know will come up. You have to learn to wait. Those private things are private for a reason. If they're part of the way the man is made up, they'll come out soon enough. If he wants you, he'll open up a little more every time the two of you are together.

Meeting Mr. Right or Mr. Right Now

There are too many women who get married to Mr. Right Now. They've dreamed all their lives of being married. The first man who tells them they're beautiful, right at the moment when their life clock is ticking in their ears, is the right one. It's funny how the "right words" are heard only when all your emotions are lined up. Marriage happens when that man is brave enough to give in to a woman's desperate cries for a husband. It's right then Mr. Right Now says, "I do!"

Who is Mr. Right Now? I just described him in the first paragraph. The emotions are aligning, he's ready, and so are you. It doesn't take long for him to ask you to marry him and the two of you are off to your future. This sounds ideal, but sometimes it doesn't work. He was Mr. Right Now because of where you both were in your life, but he doesn't know you and you don't know him. Occasionally there are fights to stay married from the very beginning. The "now" has passed, and the future is looking extremely dim.

Then there is the time when you both are in the right stages of your lives and the courtship runs smoothly. You get married, and it's working. This is when the getting-to-know-you stage presents surprise information that doesn't fade your love. You're both growing together. He's willing to compromise, and so are you. Nothing you've ever done or are doing now is a deal-breaker. No, you're not going to tolerate *anything*, but you are patient and working through *everything*. From courtship to marriage you must think deeply about what you're doing. Your contemplative thoughts turn out some good results.

> **Marriage is about sacrifice. If neither of you ever yields to the other, then you don't have a marriage**

Marriage takes sacrifice. You may consider what I'm about to say as controversial, but it must be said. Marriage is about sacrifice. If neither of you ever yields to the other, then you don't have a marriage. It's even worse if one is giving in and the other one is refusing. You still don't have a marriage.

Bibletools.com describes biblical marriage as the union of man and woman in intimacy where both complement each other in the whole of life. The problem is that many people marry for anything other than the above reason. Still, in the 21st century, some women get married because they don't want to have sex outside of the confines of the marriage. This is *a* reason. Can this reason hold up in the process of time? Will sex be enough? My answer is no. If it was the original reason, then concessions have to be made. The problem is you can marry a man who will give you good sex, but the rest of his life may not line up with your beliefs by any stretch of the imagination. You're supposed to become one in mind and spirit. Only having good sex cannot do that for you (although, it is a good start).

Here are a few examples of reasons why people might choose Mr. Right Now instead of Mr. Right:

- Rushing to get married so you can have sex
- Feeling lonely
- Tired of being single
- Seeking financial security

How do you know he's Mr. Right? One example is that he takes his time to study things when you might want to rush.

Somebody has to be the bigger person. There will be an opportunity for either or both of you to do that. Make sure you're holding onto a truth that works. You cannot make up a rule and expect blind obedience. Who are you, anyway? There are guidelines that all but guarantee a decent marriage. Making up marriage rules is not one of them. When you see your marriage slipping into the abyss, you stand up and agree with God that this will not happen.

You can overcome any of the gray areas in a marriage if you're ready to suffer a little. I would not tell you to stay with someone who has no concern for your wellbeing or someone who purposely decides you're not worth the sacrifice. What I am saying is that Mr. Right Now can turn into Mr. Right if you're willing to fight. Your suffering won't last long and your marriage will be better for it. Remember, what you put out will come back as long as you're with a giving person. Sacrifice implies the giving of something you need to receive something you need more.

I've watched too many couples stay married in the most horrendous of circumstances. He isn't Mr. Right or Mr. Right Now; he was just convenient. Some couples stay together because the Bible says, "What therefore God hath joined together, let not man put asunder" (Mark 10 KJV). How do you know if God put you two together if you didn't even acknowledge God in your courtship or marriage? No, God may not tell you who to marry, but there is peace in asking Him anyway. As you date and spend time together you'll start to blend. Can you say then that God put you two together? Not really, because when he starts making a one-hundred-and-eighty-degree turn away from you, what happened? The signs were there, but *you* didn't pay them any attention because of desperation. But he can change if he wants to, and that's up to him.

Changing from a bad thing to a good thing is in the authority of a person. If he doesn't want to change, you're wasting your time. Decide this is the state of your marriage or use other options. I Corinthians 7:15 (KJV) says, "But if the unbeliever leaves, let it be so. The brother or the sister is not bound in such circumstances; God has called us to live in peace." What does this mean? If Mr. Right or Mr. Right Now was never fully at one with you, but you married anyway, he may decide he's not going to change at all, and his presence is unbearable. Funny thing is that he may never physically leave. Most divorces are initiated by the woman (https://www.liveabout.com/why-most-divorces-are-initiated-by-women-3974044). If you're going to tolerate his emotional disconnect, he's probably not going to move. After all, why should he? He's already gone. You're just in a resting and safe place.

Think about the whole purpose of marriage. It's a symbol of how Christ loved the church. What kind of husband treats his wife badly and expects her to deal with it forever? That's a husband who knows you're not leaving. "In this same way, husbands ought to love their wives as their own bodies. He who loves his wife loves himself. [29] After all, no one ever hated their own body, but they feed and care for their body, just as Christ does the church" (Ephesians 5:28-30). Does your marriage or imagination of marriage match this scenario?

Whether you're married to Mr. Right or considering marrying Mr. Right Now, think about reconciling your thought process to the principles that make up a marriage. Your body belongs to your spouse. Somebody has got to be in charge, and God made that order be Himself, the man, and then the wife. You are to submit to him, and he is to submit to you, both for respect to God (Ephesians 5:21). He's not in charge to rule you but to cover you in love. Yes, living right can cause him to turn into Mr. Right if he's willing.

Some of you are waiting for Mr. Right, but have no idea what you're looking for, so you turn a man off after the first conversation. You may have cornered the market on success but presenting that you don't need him will never help you make a love connection. You may not need him, but you better make him feel like you do. He will be Mr. Right immediately.

Being needy isn't the same as needing a husband. Some of you are already wife material, but your neediness is covering your true assets. Decide that if you never marry you'll be fine. If you live here you have a higher chance of meeting the one who will not take advantage of you. Neediness is a handicap. Coming in with unpaid bills, unruly children, and no place to live is a sure sign of neediness. Some men long to be a savior of the universe, but when life sets in they will lose their superpowers. You should need a husband—a king—on whom you can pour all your wifely assets because you are a queen.

Mr. Right is out there looking. If you never turn into Mrs. Right, the two of you may never connect. Straighten out your crown and walk in your confidence. Whether he's Mr. Right Now today or is ready to be Mr. Right, what you bring to the table *will be* the deciding factor.

The Happy Test

In the chapter called "Answering the Question," I talked about how the joy of marriage is a foundation that will keep you married. But everyone wants to be happy; although fleeting, happiness has its purpose. Happiness is what you feel on a vacation to the Caribbean, staying on beach-front property. Happy is the emotion when all the bills are paid, and you can eat out regularly.

Happiness is a moving target, and you better shoot straight. Happiness doesn't just have an intermittent purpose; with every activity, there should be a period of happiness that follows. No matter what it is, happiness should peek through at some point. I devised something I call the Happy Test. At intervals in your relationship, you should stop everything and ask your partner if he/she is happy. This will make all the difference in the longevity you're pushing for. Although it sounds like a close-ended question, it's not. It's a question that is to act as a conversation starter. This will be a moment of open dialogue on the whole purpose of staying together. If happiness doesn't play a big part in your relationship, what are you doing? After the test is taken you both should strive to make the changes that will ensure great periods of pure happiness. If you're both shooting at the same target, it will get hit.

The happy test comprises one question: *are you happy?* The idea is to go into this territory with an open heart and the decision to do what it takes to keep your spouse happy. If the answer is yes you have to be determined to continue on this course; you're in a good place. If the answer is no, then you must be willing to do whatever it takes to make your spouse happy. Today! If you get a negative response, you then have to ask the next question: what can you do to make him/her happy?

This test should not be an opportunity to criticize your spouse to their detriment. There is a tremendous difference between plain criticism and constructive criticism. Criticism is described in Webster's Dictionary as "the act of expressing disapproval and noting the problems or faults of a person or thing." When you criticize constructively, you do it in love and look for ways to boost the chemistry between you and your lover. You are constructing a better bond.

Criticism can be painful. If you are dishing out criticism for the sole purpose of inflicting pain, then this does nothing but bring devastation to the recipient. On the other hand, if you are criticizing trying to build on a long-term relationship, your spouse has the opportunity to process the complaint about its merit and make some changes.

Keep in mind what I said. This chapter is called "The Happy Test." The two of you have decided your goal is to add all the happiness you can to each other's life. Remember that happiness comes from happenings. You want to create as many things that cause happiness as you can. This will be a joint effort, and it's worth the momentary discomfort you both may feel hearing your "faults."

The biggest deterrent to this test is pride. Who wants to be told a certain way you do something is an irritation to your spouse? The worst situation is when you decide to start working on a fault on your own and that very thing is what your spouse decides is what bothers him so much. Don't get bent out of shape. You knew it was something that needed to be fixed before he said it. Let the advice be a confirmation you were working on the right thing.

The keyword is agreed.

The purpose is to bring happiness to places where there may be adversity. If you decide to do it alone, then you have to ask your spouse how you can make him happy and not start on a campaign to beat down their ego. I guarantee you it will not end well if that is your MO.

Before starting, establishing some ground rules may help when you do this for the first time. Keeping your emotions in check may be where you want to start. If after the first criticism the discussion turns into an all-out war, then the test was an instant failure. The way you form your complaint is also something to put in place. This is not the time to explode with all of your pent-up aggression on every matter you've been afraid to mention over the past five years. You can't get all of your happiness needs to be addressed in one day, and you can always come back to some others at another time. Regularly practice open communication as a way of getting to know more about your spouse and letting him know more about you. This test isn't an answer to all your character flaws about passive-aggressiveness in how the two of you communicate. The test should be lighthearted and fun. The subject matter may sometimes be serious, but that doesn't mean that it has to be thrown out like a grenade.

Wanting to keep your spouse happy should be one of your greatest priorities. Never think so highly of yourself that one criticism bursts your bubble. All of a sudden, your demeanor changes, and you ready yourself with every bit of ammunition you can muster. Happiness is relative. Just because *you* think cheese with every meal should make your spouse ecstatic and you find out it doesn't mean your $15.75-an-ounce fine cheese was bad; it's just not what your spouse likes. If she likes Olive Garden better than Red Lobster and tells you this after two years of going every week, don't despair.

Having a tantrum because your feelings are hurt won't solve anything. No one will be made happy by this action. You'll take her out again, and you'll either go to Olive Garden or you will compromise on a place you both like.

As the years pass by and the two of you get more connected, it'll become easier and the test may soon fade into the past. As you learn each other's likes and dislikes, your daily actions will lean more and more in favor of your spouse. You won't have to hear your wife tell you picking your teeth at the table grosses her out. When you raise your pinky finger to get the meat out of your back molar, in your head you'll hear her say, *Honey, when you pick your teeth while we're eating I lose my appetite!* You'll lower your hand from the side of your head and excuse yourself for a moment. It'll become that simple.

Building a life together takes work. If you're willing to make small changes along the way it'll soon become a mission of yours. I can almost guarantee the energy you expend to make your spouse happy will be reciprocated in ways that far outweigh your minor adjustments.

Do some happy testing and do the requested work. Some of the changes are long overdue and you'll be better for it. If you've only been on one vacation in five years or maybe none, saving money may be a new "hobby" for you. Any change for the better is a plus for both of you. Not only will you be making your spouse happy, but you'll raise your net worth in his or her eyes. You have nothing to lose!

Cut the Cord

What do you know about making a happy home but what you saw at home, read about, or saw in the movies? You get married and think you can dictate the direction of your house by what you think you know. "Mom used to, so I do too." "Dad used to, so I have to." But I'm here to show you there's a better way that's the right way; the godly way.

When a woman is in labor, she's told to push until that baby's head comes out and then the doctor or midwife begins helping the baby make its entrance into a whole new world. A world where he/she will have to start breathing on their own and sucking from a bottle to receive their nutrients. Then as the child becomes an adult, they'll eventually leave home and start their own family. All of this is a normal progression, but one step was missed—after the baby is fully out of the mother's womb the doctor has to do a final separation of the mother and child. The umbilical cord must be cut. This cord carried oxygenated, nutrient-rich blood from the mother to the unborn child. This is how the child survived inside the mother during the pregnancy. The cutting of the cord signifies the beginning of the child's independence from the mother.

Of course, this cord is a physical cord, but the attachment you have to your family remains long after delivery. This is where many problems can occur in a relationship if an adult does not make the purposeful decision to cut the familial cord that can hinder the growth of a new family system.

In the Bible, when Moses was born his mother put him in a basket and set him in the river, saving him from the Egyptians who wanted all baby boys born to the Israelite slaves killed. He was found by the Pharaoh's daughter and raised as her own child (story can be found in Exodus 2).

At forty years old Moses fled away from his familiar surroundings to begin a legacy separate from what he was used to. His purpose would be totally opposite of the one to which he was used to. He would be gone for forty years and return as the man who would lead the Israelites out of slavery. But this only happened after he was gone for forty years from his childhood home.

This concept is repeated in the life of Abraham (previously Abram, meaning the high father) who would be instructed by God to leave the home of his father and all relatives. He would go from the patriarch of his family to the father of many nations (Genesis 12). The cord had to be cut from both of these men. Instructions for starting a new legacy have not changed. Since the beginning, in Genesis 2:24 the man is told to leave his mother and father and cleave or hold on to his wife. Then it says the two will become one. The main words to focus on here are "to become."

It's not an easy task to take two people from two entirely different backgrounds and have them work to become one, unified in thought and heart. It's nearly impossible if one or both of them is still holding on or attached to the cord of their birth home. You might think cutting the cord is saying the old value system is wrong, but this isn't true. It's different and worked in the previous house. The union is just new and needs its own blended value system.

In the 1960s television series *Star Trek*, one alien character, Spock, was from the fictional planet Vulcan. His mind was said to be melded with another man from Vulcan. In this so-called melding, a person could telepathically share thoughts with another human. In the real world, this is not the way day-to-day life occurs. And a wife can't expect her husband to understand what old habits are killing the relationship unless she opens her mouth. Her passive-aggressive behavior or condescending words will never begin to cut the cord of what he's doing and vice versa.

Your mom may have cooked chicken every Friday, but your husband is used to fish. Your response to a request for fish should not be, "My mother cooked chicken every Friday, and that's not a tradition I want to break. You just have to get over it!" My suggestion would be to plan a different meal together, go out on Fridays, or just eat pizza! But stubbornness by either spouse is just plain ol' dysfunction. If you want to foster a peaceful atmosphere you have to kill the dysfunction. It's the small stuff that messes things up. The universal principles you learned at home, on the playground, or in high school are transferrable into adulthood in your marriage. But everything you learned in those places does best staying in those places. Mommy's fish was good, but it may not be the best for your new family setting.

There are many cords we might have to cut, not just with our parents but also with relationships.

Your girlfriends told you that you better hide money from your man so he won't spend it all. So here you are twenty years later watching your man work three jobs, paying the majority of the bills alone, while you sneak off on Saturdays with your girls enjoying life. You have a hidden stash of money you pinch off when you get ready. You must think he's stupid. Who told you that? Which one of your "unmarried" girlfriends did this work for? Your stash can be for that time you decide to surprise him with something he never thought you could afford!

How about some unified thinking about saving? Maybe you both decide to save five dollars a week. You say that's not much. Well, fives turn into tens, and tens into twenties. In five years you could have $3,000 in savings if you make the decision to invest together. That's a legacy you may not have been accustomed to in the house where you grew up. Okay, so you're a millionaire. Same principle applies, just a higher figure for investing and return on investment.

Get on the same page about your life together. Those "first truths" you were raised with may not work in your present home.

Your mother may have used sex as a tool. When she and your father got into a dispute he was starved in the bedroom. You knew it because his attitude was out of whack the next day. You may have heard the yelling at night when he threatened to go get "it" from somewhere else. That manipulation stayed in control until divorce was the only answer. Is that the same result you're working on? That "same page" work can take you through the rest of your life together.

There are two things I believe couples planning to marry should never neglect to talk about. You should get pre-marital counseling, but even if you don't, please talk about this: sex and money. If you know you think sex is nasty because your mother told you it was, you need help. You are marrying a man who was told he should have sex whenever and however he wanted it. You both are headed for a collision. Talk about it way before saying, "I do!" The other topic of money is an extremely important one. It's the most common subject in the Bible, mentioned over eight hundred times (http://www.forbes.com/sites/sherylnancenash). Money is also the biggest contributor for marriage breakups (http://www.jrn.com/ktnv).

The contract of the hearts is the biggest influence of how you will agree to a peaceful and prosperous home. When I started in ministry I did not have a dollar, but I planned to prosper. Although now divorced, my union was definitely one of living life in abundance. A lack of financial planning can contribute to chaos at home. "Money answers all things" (Ecclesiastes 10:19). Make one of your foundational values be that of honesty in finances.

Some of you may have seen the struggles in the house where you were raised, but how to change the habits has not been the foundation of your search for a difference. Your parents did the best they could considering the information they were working with. You could and should do better. Decide to cut the cord. You're intelligent enough to make the necessary changes that will afford you a great legacy.

When you're doing something that aggravates your spouse, choose to get to the source of the reason for your habit. I can almost guarantee you'll trace it back to "first truths" you were taught before you got married. These foundations must be broken, and new ones formed. You must be willing to change.

Cutting the cord doesn't mean you'll stop interacting with your blood relatives, but it does mean their influence on your bad habits will be destroyed. The direction for you and your spouse is a private one. You do not need your mama's, daddy's, or auntie's approval. You are now grown and have to put away childish ways (I Corinthians 13:11). Your mother's wisdom is still good, but her opinion has no business infiltrating the unified minds of you and your spouse.

It's hard to be wrong. The way you handle some things may be out of habit. When your spouse suggests another way, calling your mom as an ally is counterproductive. What's she going to do, come to your house and straighten out your husband? Stop thinking about everything in terms of right and wrong. How about just different?

You don't have to be that perfect mother, expert wife, and superb help. It's this concept of perfect that has messed up many marriages. Your best is all you can do. If your best is not always criticized, then stop reacting when something isn't quite right. Just because in your childhood home your dad played catch with your brother, does that mean your husband has to do the same? Nagging your husband because he doesn't do what you expect him to do doesn't make your home any less perfect than what you were raised in. You're his wife, not his mother.

Life is not meant to be so rigid. If you would just relax, you'd be surprised what will happen. Block out all the noise of what you're so used to hearing. You're married now, or going to be. Listen to the sound of *your* marriage. What is it saying? You'll find your husband is hearing many of the same sounds and words. Rest into it and blend. This is now Mr. and Mrs. New Name, not the

House of Maiden Name. There's no forcing in a union when two people are pliable.

You're now becoming one with your spouse and what he thinks or says does make a difference in how your home is run. You be the difference that you want to see. Do not let the mistakes of your parents be your mistakes too. Cut the cord!

DNA is not Enough

Many different types of people get married. Some spouses have been married before, single fathers, single mothers, and the traditional first-timers with no children. In this chapter, we'll discuss the blended family.

"The simple definition of a blended family, also called a stepfamily, reconstituted family, or a complex family, is a family unit where one or both parents have children from a previous relationship, but they have combined to form a new family" (www.Needtoknow.com). Although one word describing this kind of union is complex, I want to bring some light to these unions and finally start a rally to do away with the wrong connotation of the word "step"; this will automatically make the word complex here a misstatement. The word "step" could be used and add pain to a child already struggling to fit in during settlement into a new family dynamic. A child cannot be expected to blend on their own terms.

I've seen the demeanor of young children change as a parent introduces several children when one or more happen to be stepchildren. It was like a step down had to be taken to include them. What is a step, anyway? Step as used in the word "stepchild" derives from the Old English word *steopcild*, meaning orphan. This was saying a child was bereaving the death of his parents (www.bonusfamilies.com). The definition of an orphan is a child who has no parents. Of course, this word was originally from back in 800 AD, but it was never changed and is still used today. But the word doesn't have to have a negative connotation. The word in the 21st century doesn't mean orphan. Words have power. Using the word "step" with the wrong connotation is incorrect, like any adjective used to introduce anyone: "my used-to-be friend," "my hated baby daddy," "the boss who fired me."

Like everything else, words take on new meanings and definitions get added in the dictionary. "Stepchild" today doesn't mean an orphaned child, but if a stepparent shows no love to his non-biological child or feels differently towards her or him, then the child may feel orphaned. If a child is coming from a divorce situation, that's already painful enough without a stepparent rejecting a child. It must be understood that you as a stepparent must gain the love and respect of this new child. This is *your* responsibility and not vice versa. More children come from single mothers because of a decline in marriage (https://www.pewresearch.org/fact-tank/2018/04/27/about-one-third-of-u-s-children-are-living-with-an-unmarried-parent/). You have to consider this when discussing how a child became a stepchild. Either way, a child is engrafted in, the child's healthy, loving relationship with his caregivers must be considered. Consider a child in a blended family, not an orphan, as was originally meant.

In Ephesians 1, God adopted all believers from the foundation of the world. No one did anything to deserve God as the father, but through His love and grace, He has drawn you in. It was by His good pleasure. It was by the Blood of Jesus that all became sons and daughters of God. God has no favorites; He loves us all the same. By Jesus's death and resurrection, all are adopted. Some synonyms for adoption are acceptance, appropriation, approval, endorsement, maintenance, and selection. All these words match what God did for you even in your worst state. He reached down and rescued you from a life destined for failure. If God did that for you why would you treat a child added to your family as anything but one of your own? God didn't keep from you all the promises He gave others. Jesus was designated as different by way of the Holy Spirit but was known as the son of Joseph and Mary (Matthew 13:55). His earthly father was Joseph and definitely not by blood.

His birth and life were too important to entrust to a human father. Nonetheless, where He grew up He was known as one of the siblings in His earthly family. He was fully engrafted in, and in that became known as a descendant of King David as a son of Joseph (Matthew 1:18-25).

DNA is the building block for all life forms. DNA gives you your looks, genetic makeup, and earthly bloodline. But it has nothing to do with the way you live your life. The way of living comes from spiritual impartation and experiences. God knew that when He sent Jesus. If you could have done it on your own, Jesus wouldn't have come. You may have been raised by your father, or you may have never known him. Neither of those things is necessarily the determining factor as to how you turned out. If absentee fathers or deadbeat dads were the foundation for all failure, then you're looking at a miracle of all those successful people who grew up in single-parent, matriarchal households.

DNA does not determine your religion or whether you will become a doctor, lawyer, teacher, or social worker. You may have decided to choose those fields because you saw a relative work in them, but that was not a guarantee. If it were the reason, then all sons having a deadbeat father are destined to repeat the same behavior. But some men are excellent fathers and never knew their fathers.

The spirit is more powerful than DNA. The right to be adopted into God's spiritual family could not be entrusted to man's blood. He used the Holy Spirit to impregnate Virgin Mary. This is called the Immaculate Conception. It was called "immaculate," meaning unblemished, perfect, untainted, etc. Because of man's original sin, God didn't want to take the chance of ruining a perfect design of salvation by bringing the savior through natural conception. He did it Himself, thereby giving everyone a right to come into His kingdom. It is not DNA that gives you the right but the Spirit of God that comes in you and joins with your spirit, giving you the power to be adopted. That's how you are saved by faith. You just have to accept it.

In Deuteronomy 7 God proclaims Israel (the Jewish nation) as His chosen people. In the Old Testament, you can read of all the miracles performed for them even when they were disobedient. They stand as an example to us of God's goodness and promises set for the world that is pronounced to everyone in the New Testament (Galatians 3). The adoption for all believers is reiterated throughout these verses. You may not be from the Jewish bloodline but have been engrafted to obtain the same promises (Romans 11).

This is the same concept that should be employed when marrying with children already here. The children should be adopted in and blended as if they came from the same source. Your spirit is what will make the difference. Children coming into a family who has both natural and "adopted" parents involved in their lives should be considered favored because this is a blessing. These children have a wealth of knowledge coming from several directions. The parents of these children have agreed to work together whether through meetings or in their actions. Developing this kind of working relationship should be addressed early or before marriage. It can and does work (www.apa.org). The big adjustment should come through the children, not the adults because they're not making the choice.

Your job is to nurture all of your children. There is no way that God expects a difference between "adopted" and naturally born children. Your influence will do more to direct his/her steps in life if you do not differentiate. This is the thought I want you to consider when it comes to raising children who happen not to have your DNA.

If you practice embracing the child as your own you'll soon see there's no difference in the favor God shows from one child to the next. DNA cannot do that. Rejection causes problems for any child, adopted or born. You wouldn't want to look back ten years from now and realize that only God's favor raised the level of your "adopted" child's life. It happens regardless; you may as well participate. Children are a blessing and a heritage. Your spiritual impartation is designed by God for the children who live in your house.

Psychologists say stepparents should reserve disciplining age-appropriate children until after the first year of marriage. Building a loving connection should be the first priority. Children may resent the proposed or imagined state of replacing a natural parent and care should be taken to realize this may be an issue (www.apa.org). This is something you should consider and discuss as you determine if God told you to get married.

It doesn't matter what kind of atmosphere to which a child has been accustomed; your spiritual influence will make all the difference. You cannot do it like a drill sergeant, but with the love of God. Your goal should never be to prove how much "better" you are than a natural parent (even if it's true) because you'll only add to the resentment a child already has toward you.

You may have watched children from extremely dysfunctional homes turn to drugs and street life. You probably automatically thought, DNA. But I'm telling you this wasn't the only cause. DNA plays a part in genetic makeup, but it's not the determining factor of how a child will turn out. The answer is learned behavior. That's why what a parent does is much more important than what he or she says.

The Bible's entire theme is about your relationship with God and with other people. That's because your relationship with God defines how you'll treat other people. This is why how you treat your children and train them is more potent than how you're physically related to them. God knew He had to direct us on how to love others. He gave you that same power to affect the lives of all of your children.

The children brought into the marriage by your spouse are not orphans. They came as a package deal, and it's a job God knew *you* could handle, just like God knew Joseph could handle raising Jesus.

They need your love and supportive influence and not your aversion to their DNA. DNA has nothing to do with it. It brought them here, but how they end up depends on your decision to give just like they came through you. Give the children time to get used to you during the dating season and once you take your position in the house.

It's not the last name but the spirit of the man that makes the difference. This entire concept needs to be redefined. When a man marries a woman with children—or vice versa—he's marrying her *and* her children. It's a set that cannot be broken up. Start resenting your husband's children and watch the change happen. He'll start resenting you. If he doesn't get through to you with his concerns, he'll look for the affirmation from elsewhere. These children are his, and if you resent them you resent part of him.

Some situations might lead to resentment. Don't let your resentment of him or his children be one of them. This might cause him to cheat on you. I'm not justifying it but giving you a fact that may help you decide to make all the adjustments you need to fix problems. You have to kill the root of many of the attitudes that show themselves in your house. Although many words may not be spoken on the subject, the actions will speak louder than words, so pay attention.

The children coming into a marriage should be referred to in an endearing way. You cannot fake how you feel because it's going to show. After developing the right relationship discuss how you and the children will be addressed. If the word "step" is used it should be with the most love and affection just as you speak of your natural children. You want to foster the right behavior and must share your love from the heart. Children sometimes know the difference before adults and on occasion when adults have no clue.

If you're not married yet, consider what you're reading here. If you're already married decide to do the fine-tuning necessary for a better home life for your children. Your love and attention can make all the difference to that child who comes in with abandonment issues. Everyone wants to be loved and accepted. Remember one synonym for adoption is maintenance. Children need to be maintained until they reach the age of maturity and can fend for themselves. They're here for a reason, and that should be their only job, seeking out their purpose and fulfilling it. They shouldn't have to spend the bulk of their time looking for love and acceptance everywhere else but in their own home.

You have the power to change, if necessary, the natural propensity of a child to act like his or her birth parent. You can change the course of nature. Spending quality time to ensure all your children are loved, trained, and shown the road to a successful life can override any dysfunctional "generational curses" that seek to repeat in their generation. On the other hand, your job may simply be to reinforce what the child learned or is learning from his natural parent.

Some parents have had to break away from their blood relatives to give their child the opportunity to change the course of "nature" that has been ruling for generations. But God has promised mothers and sisters and brothers that can fill the void left by this departure (Mark 10). If God knew this transition worked, who are you to decide otherwise? Accept the job God is giving you. Be the other mother who can give that added covering to a child looking for love and direction.

When God made man He made him in the likeness and image of Himself (Genesis 1:26). The human spirit is the part of man created like God. The human spirit is spirit and not flesh and blood. The human spirit is greater than DNA. It can be formed and cultivated to direct a life into the perfect design to fulfill its purpose.

"A good man leaves an inheritance to his children's children" (Proverbs 13:22). This is a passage that should be incorporated before getting married. All the children should be considered and placed in the right perspective in family heritage. You can't do anything about what blood a child was born with, but you can decide to make any attitude adjustments necessary to help a child make an easy transition into new surroundings. You can do what it takes to give correct spiritual life formation. Who is this child to you? Is he/she part of your spouse? Is he/she worth your energy to impart principles that will direct him/her into great productivity in life?

God didn't make a mistake by putting Mary with Joseph. Did God tell Joseph to marry Mary? Not initially. But when she was found to be pregnant, God did affirm to Joseph she was still going to be his wife. The backstory is that God did arrange this marriage. The Messiah was prophesied as coming from the line of David (Isaiah 11:1). The line was an anointed one. God does not make mistakes, not with Jesus and not with that child you may have to mother who didn't come from your womb.

There are no perfect marriages, but some families are striving to maintain a foundation that will send productive citizens into the world. Your children should be no different and should be afforded all the opportunities you can deliver. Embrace all your children the same and give out your love equally. You'll grow to accept all of them the same and be rewarded by the success you see developing as they mature. It will be well worth the effort and your time.

Functional and Dysfunction in Families

All families are dysfunctional! No family exists on earth that functions perfectly the way families were meant to function by design. This is a true statement now and was true since the beginning of time. The first family ever to live in the world brought dysfunction to every family that would come after.

All humans come into the world naturally craving necessities. Infants cry if they're not held, fed, or protected. Babies don't like loud noises or pain and can perceive when they're not loved. These needs never change. When individuals are missing these basic needs dysfunction occurs, maintained by the emotional trauma that many times accompanies the neglect.

You're probably picturing children running around in dirty clothes with runny noses, and parents fighting in the living room paying no attention to the children crying in the bedroom. That may be an extreme case, but dysfunction happens with varying severity in households across the world. How much occurs in your house, only you can answer.

Why does it happen? One way is generational. Parents model what they saw and went through in the place where they were raised. You get mad and throw dishes at the wall when you're the one who has to clean it up and replace them, only because your mama did the same thing. You accept physical abuse from your husband because you watched your mother get hit by your dad and stay with him without any intervention, all while saying she knows he loves her.

You keep doing wrong and expecting right to come out of it. Is there really a thing called a generational curse? Your dad smoked crack to ease the pain of life's downfalls, so you escape in the bottle. It's a cycle. The curse isn't somebody cooking a brew in a big kettle with a chant; it's as simple as a generationally repeated offense that needs somebody to say, "It ends here!" No good is ever going to come out of it if no one decides to make the change.

The Book of Genesis in the second through fourth chapters tells the story of Adam and Eve. It relays their failures and subsequent first child's problems. A few lines into the fourth chapter, Cain kills his brother Abel. The reason was jealousy. Then Cain believes that blaming his brother for his bad attitude will solve his issue. This wasn't new territory in the Scripture. Adam, Cain's dad, had done the same thing before. He blamed his wife for his downfall. When Cain was corrected by God for his bad attitude he took it out on his brother.

The dilemma of dysfunction lives on. Is your family dysfunctional? If you're honest, your answer will be yes. It's so amazing how people see the dysfunction in their families yet still expect their families to operate perfectly. They don't understand dysfunction as a flaw in function. Just about every predicament that falls on a family results from the same dysfunction that interrupts every peaceful season. The confusion lies in the fact that to embrace and correct the flaws you have to admit they exist. You can't fix what you refuse to acknowledge.

I don't want you to expand your thoughts beyond your immediate family. Don't include Uncle John who you know is a closet alcoholic or Aunt Susie who gambles away her mortgage regularly. It's so easy to look at extended family and see the mess but right in your house, under your roof, is a picture of similar dysfunction. Some actions still take place because of what was modeled in front of you. You leave home intending to leave behind those things you couldn't stand. You come to yourself and realize you have repeated many of those same things you hated growing up.

The first step for change is to understand you cannot change anyone but yourself. You have to admit you need a change. Living in denial or blaming your spouse or *all* the men you meet as your date is mere fantasy. There is but one common denominator, and that is you! You can decide that it will be different, or you can remain a victim, living like there's no way out.

One definition of "functional" is having a special activity, purpose, or task; relating to how something works or operates.

You have to have a paradigm shift. A paradigm is a model of how something is supposed to work. You want a complete change, you must install a brand-new model. "For every action, there is an equal and opposite reaction," wrote the mathematician Sir Isaac Newton. Reconcile this with your current family situation and start thinking of what new actions may need to be put into place. Don't try to make changes where you have no authority. You can only change yourself so your actions must be personal. "I know he's acting crazy and needs some adjustments." But that isn't the right thought because you cannot force that action. You can start acting on what you can change and see the equal or opposite reaction occur. This is not about him, but about your issues. If he never changes, you *still* will come out a better person.

In counseling, it is called "peeling the layers" (www.pyschologicalassoc.com). As you begin to take a look at your actions and discover a hidden agenda, the way you're responding has little to do with what is happening right now. For example, your husband comes back from the grocery store five minutes past the time *you* calculated, and you go into a rage. If you dig you will realize your last husband was a regular cheater, or your daddy had an entire other family on the other side of town and regularly made trips to the corner store that took two hours. Now, your poor husband must be punished for all the hurt you encountered at the hands of those other men.

You get jealous of how your sister's husband can shower her with expensive gifts, so you start pressuring your husband to step up his game. It's human nature to be jealous. You have to learn how to manage it. You may have come from a family that kept up with the infamous Joneses. Jealousy does not have to rule your life; it can be managed. When jealousy calls, don't answer. Stop comparing yourself to others. Let the Joneses live their life and you live yours. Make your way the "it" thing.

Generational curses have no power when you acknowledge they exist and do something about them. This dysfunction can lead to many things greater than the manifested actions. Drug addiction is sometimes the escape of choice only for the addict to come down from the high to face the problem that never went anywhere. Then the cycle continues.

> **Generational curses have no power when you acknowledge they exist and do something about them**

You can't fix your family issues by controlling them. Hollering and screaming or using manipulation never changed anything. You can't stop your husband from hanging out by badgering him every time he comes home or by withholding sex when you don't get your way. Whipping your child into submission when he/she misbehaves in school will solve nothing if he/she comes home every day to an unkempt house and has to scrounge around to find something to eat. You fix problems by applying the proper principles of order.

You may have grown up in foster care, without a father, an absent mother, or been adopted. None of this catches God by surprise. In the first chapter of Jeremiah God tells Jeremiah that He knew him before he was formed in his mother's womb (Jeremiah 1:5). That statement is true for every person who lives or ever lived.

Your Creator knew you before you were born and knows you right now.

Every created being also was created with a purpose. You may have many purposes: mother, sister, teacher, aunt, friend, etc. How you fulfill your purpose depends on how much you're in touch with your creator. If you want to know how something works or is made, the best place to get that information is its maker.

Since you were formed by God, He is the one who has the blueprint. To correct deficiencies, going back to the original blueprint will give you a picture of what the original plan looked like. He holds the master plan and gives you the power (Acts 1:8) to return to that plan whenever you veer off course. You can find a way to correct every deficit if you are looking.

You may be wondering if it's that simple, why hasn't someone in your lineage done it before now? That's a powerful question. But God in His infinite wisdom planned for this information to fall into your hands right this moment as you are reading this. You do not have to go under the knife for nine hours to get fixed. The wisdom from God is right here for you. Like the old cliché says, "When the student is ready, the teacher will appear" (an old religious Proverb). This is the place you're in today. You are ready for a change.

God knows you need help to get through all the tangles of this life. That's why he sent His son, Jesus Christ, and ultimately the great comforter, the Holy Spirit. Now you have access to the correct principles to straighten out your life. Not only do you have correct principles, but you have the power to overcome those areas of your life that keep you hurt and confused.

It's never easy to admit you contribute to the dysfunction of your family. But that's a freeing truth worth going through the slight discomfort of your change to add to the positive function of your family. Only you can change yourself. *You* cannot change anybody else and nobody can change *you* but *you*!

Decide today that you will seek out those principles that can change your family dynamics. Just because you were never hugged doesn't mean you can't learn to hug and love your children. Just because you never witnessed adult affection at home does not mean you can't begin giving affection. With the power inside you, you can learn how to forgive the parent you may feel wronged you and move on to living as you are purposed to do before the foundation of the world.

The power can help you get a makeover that will teach you to trust God and not be constantly afraid of your spouse or every man you meet doing you wrong. Your earthly father may have been absent or never modeled love, trust, and support to his family. But with the help of God, you will begin to embrace change and start giving your best. You will no longer project the pain you grew up with onto everyone who tries to get close to you. You will realize its source and forgive the past.

Healthy families do not have to be found on TV. You can look forward to sowing the right seeds in your family and looking for healthy returns. You change, and change will take place. I have seen it happen before; one person changes and the other spouse makes a turn-in response. Decide that your family will be the poster family for the families in your neighborhood, church, and surrounding communities.

You   be   the   change   you   want   to   see.

Friends with Benefits

riends with Benefits is a 2011 film starring Justin Timberlake and Mila Kunis. The two characters are best friends and decide to add romantic flings to their relationship, believing it won't change the dynamics of it. Of course, it does. This concept struck a chord with me while writing this book. Why can't a married couple be friends? If you ask a married person who his best friend is you may hear it's his wife. But this is not common. Many married people maintain close relationships outside of marriage and that is not a problem. But what would happen if people contemplating marriage considered this as part of the setup? They don't have to get rid of all their other friends; that's not the point. They could be that friend with benefits.

> **The friendship is the blessing and the marriage and everything else is a benefit**

Can you imagine the benefits of being married to your friend and enjoying the friendship along with the dating? The bonus is being married. You're best friends first, then you're husband and wife—everything else is a benefit. Friendship is the blessing and marriage and everything else is a benefit. To get married to your friend sounds great, but if you're simply just dating, you'll have to make the effort in courtship to become friends.

If you are a person inclined to make friends, doing this with your future husband may not be so hard. There are too many married people who have nothing in common except a house, some kids, and the bills. What's so great about that? Finding something in common is not so hard. If you both are human and live on this planet, there must be something you both like to do. Your dating life shouldn't just consist of doing that traditional thing of trying to impress each other or adding outings neither of you particularly enjoy. What kind of things do you do with your other "best" friend(s)?

If you take adding this element into consideration, you may find it's the best thing you can do for a lasting relationship. Even when things get bumpy, you can rely on your friendship to keep everything in perspective. It's funny how much you can tolerate from a friend that you can't tolerate from the one you share a bed with. Friends fight and make up, go a week without speaking and find a way to make that call, and plan outings they both enjoy. How about making a new friend first and then adding the benefits?

I believe the lack of friendship in a marriage is one of the reasons communication is sometimes difficult. If your friend told you to adjust your weave, you would probably thank her. But, let your husband say that on the wrong day and it may turn into an all-out war, especially if he left the toilet seat up this morning and you sat down on the bare rim. Just like the friends you already have, you can confide in your husband if you've made a lasting friendship.

You don't kick a friend to the curb if she forgets your birthday. You may tell her you're mad for the moment, but that's the extent. Proverbs 17:17 says that friends stay loving each other, and just like a brother, they stick around when troubles come. This verse notes that this kind of brother is "born for adversity." That's why God cherishes relationships. The unity of people who are believers is how the world knows you follow Christ. Forgetting a birthday is a small thing for someone you love and call your friend.

What better relationship can you have than a lifetime with a friend? Too many people go into relationships with expectations that can never be fulfilled. A husband is no less human than your mother. You may have your list of wants in a spouse, but you'll always have that hidden agenda that pops up piece by piece and at the worst times. This isn't the activity of a friend. Friends find a common bond that keeps them close. What you hear from the fighting in a marriage are suppressed desires that rear their heads during a heated debate. All of a sudden you're thinking about the broken promises. You envision all of the unfulfilled desires you had hidden in the back of your mind but never asked for. You cover the defects of your closest lifelong friends, but your husband or boyfriend is supposed to be perfect. Most of that can be skipped if you make an effort to let the nuances of friendship develop as you grow more in love.

What do you want from marriage? The first marriage was set up because God determined it wasn't good for a man to be alone. God gave the man a helper. All you pro-women's-movement people, don't get on the wrong side of this information. A helper has big power; they can turn the world on its heels. Remind yourself of what Eve did in the Garden. The entire course of nature changed with the first act of disobedience initiated by a woman. Since that's the case, what about a woman making decisions for her family to prosper? Women carry more weight than they even understand. You must understand these principles when you enter the relationship called marriage. The practical things you want out of a marriage can be more readily obtained if you consider your man your friend.

Some women know who they are, but too many do not. A wife who is close friends with her husband will not only seek his happiness but will be fulfilled by doing her best to complete his dreams because they include her. All of this creativity is developed over time, a lifetime, to be exact. A couple grows into a lifelong partnership. Women hold a very important key to making a marriage work. Even some things men call deal-breakers can be overcome with the mental fortitude of a woman who knows why she is here and whose man is one of her best friends.

What do you expect from your best friend? You've heard the term "fair-weather friends." I consider that kind of friend not a friend. A friend does not turn his or her back when bad roads get bumpier. This is when a friend jumps into action. A friend in a relationship who is out as soon as the waters are choppy is merely an associate and a distant one at that. You do not expect much from someone you only associate with. There is no friendship. The true definition of a real friend is someone who is there through the good and bad. A friend/brother is also there to support when times are hard. Who needs a friend just for company in happy times?

Can you imagine if everyone went into a marriage with a lifetime friendship in mind? I know the original term "friends with benefits" was a connection that thrived in secrecy. But when you pick up the concept and put it squarely in the middle of a solid marriage you cannot achieve anything but success. A lifetime friendship with public benefits is a real marriage.

There's so much more to being friends with the benefit of marriage. You get communication and a shoulder to lean on. You get children you both want and who are covered under the umbrella of a solid unit; you have an automatic vacation partner; you get to share top-quality cars; and if you do it right. you can benefit from each other's retirement plans.

There's so much more to the benefits of marrying your friend. Take "friends with benefits" out of a movie fantasy and place it as the foundation of a top-notch marriage. Jesus died for His friends (John 15:13). If marriage is supposed to be a metaphor of how Christ loves His church (Ephesians 5:31, then why can't it include friendship?

Let There Be Sex Part I

I have been in church all of my life, and still, to this day I believe the church has done a poor job of talking about human sexuality. I've heard many teachings on sexual relations and at its best, the teaching is sometimes vague and too deep. Sex does have a spiritual benefit, but the act itself cannot be completed in the spiritual world. For sexual intercourse to take place a man and woman must be physically joined. Sex is not sinning. No matter what you may have heard in church or how holy you try to be, sex got the majority of you here (test-tube babies are the exception; no clones available that I know about!).

Those who still act like sex is all spiritual are lying to themselves and others (most likely just lying to others). Just because someone walks around wearing a long dress with no makeup and does not believe in permed or dyed hair doesn't take away their urge to have sex. Even women looking like this can get pregnant, and the men looking staunch are getting them pregnant. All kinds of people like to do it: the usher, the sinner, the preacher, and the missionary alike.

Many of you may have been taught sex is nasty. But to help you out, let me say sex is not nasty. Nasty is a trash can that hasn't been emptied, sitting out in the hot sun being swarmed by flies. *That's* nasty! Sex does not compare with anything like that. It is nasty, but it is nice-nasty. You cannot psych yourself into disliking sex because your grandma told you it was nasty. No matter what you were taught or how conservative you try to be, it does not take away your urge to have sex.

Do you know why you naturally want sex? It's because God created sex. You may live your life holding onto those old ways of thinking, but at the same time beneath all that frigid body is a longing for what comes naturally. God made sex, and sex is good.

You may have had an unfortunate introduction to sex, and it has created a wrong belief about it. I'm sorry this happened, but the power of God can free you from any wrong thinking about sex. Sex was not meant to be a torment to your mind. Sex between two people in love is a beautiful thing.

One of the first purposes for sex is to procreate (Genesis 1:28). God told the first couple "to be fruitful and multiply." But to procreate, sex has to take place. God gets joy out of you enjoying what He has put here for you to enjoy.

God is not going to come down from heaven and force you to enjoy all of life's benefits He has created for you. If you choose to miss the freeing sensation that comes with having God-ordained sex, then no one on this earth can fix that for you.

An excellent reason for good sex is for the gratification of two married people becoming one and enjoying each other's bodies. The only way to make sure a marriage is legally binding is when it is consummated; that means the man and wife must have sex. One way to have a marriage quickly annulled is to never come together in bed. It will be as if the marriage never happened. That marriage can officially be erased with no recourse if sex doesn't happen. The bond is not complete without sex. After a year or more of marriage without sex, a spouse can file for desertion. A couple can stay married without sex but either party can rightfully get out and owe nothing if no sex ever took place. I'm not condoning leaving your spouse, nor am I giving anyone a greenlight to divorce. However, I am stating bold truth so you understand the importance of sex in marriage.

The third reason for sex is for pleasure. This reason, for the most part, escapes the teaching that comes from many pulpits. God meant for married couples to have satisfying sex (Song of Solomon 7; Proverbs 5). Sex before marriage is called fornication, which is the sexual act performed by two people who are not married. All three of sex's purposes stated above are meant to happen during a marriage. The reason for many sexual problems can be traced back to what happened before marriage.

Back in the 1960s, girls used to whisper and talk about the girl in the neighborhood who everyone knew was not a virgin. Today, the opposite is the case. As of 2012, 95% of married people were not virgins when they married (www.waitingtillmarriage.org). The difficulty with not being a virgin is more than it is a sin, although that is true. The problem is something I call the sin of the first experience. That is something I know about because of my previous lifestyle. Sex is not sinning, but anything taken out of its perfect context can fit into the description of sin. All that sex before marriage sometimes leaves a spouse the burden of matching a personally extraordinary previous experience.

First experiences, porn, and explicit novels all add to misconceptions about what to expect in the marriage bed. Some incorrectly believe God said to save sex for marriage because He wanted to control you and keep something from you. That's the same mistake made by Adam and Eve in the Garden of Eden. They mistakenly believed the lie that God was keeping them from the Tree of Knowledge because He did not want them to know how He operated. But in reality, just like with sex He is working to protect you from the knowledge that can harm you in the future. Misconceptions only serve to give you false ideas.

God is interested in your future. He loves you and wants what is best for His creation. All the other experiences haunt your present if you do not come to yourself and confess the truth; let God erase the stain of those familiarities. No one man can fulfill all that you have practiced before you were married. Porn is even worse because those participants are acting. You have no idea how many takes it took to get that woman to look perfect under that light. God meant for couples to satisfy their sexual appetites together. Through practice, love, passion, and exploration you learn each other without interference from prior bedroom escapades. You are to learn what your spouse likes and find what you enjoy as you become one, as was designed by the Creator Himself.

There aren't as many virgins as experienced people, but virgins are a high-priced commodity. Okay, you have a (little) experience under your belt. You still have the opportunity to offer a man a chaste body, even your husband. Coming into the bedroom like a seasoned sex maniac may not be what your husband is looking for. He wants someone willing to please him and be pleased with him. Put on your best female innocence and be willing to let him know how much you love him. In return, he will do the same. No one has experience at birth.

If your lost virginity was because of an abusive experience, know you can overcome anything with the help of God. If this experience e is causing you shame or pain know you do not have to go through life flawed. God can and will take away the shame of your youth (Isaiah 54:4).

If you are having issues in the bedroom, you must research the cause because this can be a deal-breaker. Whether married, single, or divorced, sex is a viable part of life. It is good to know what should be expected well in advance. You married folks should take this information with you on your next encounter. If you believe you need professional counseling in this area, get some. Sexual inadequacies don't have to be a problem if you're willing to do the work.

You have to know that as a married woman you were put here to please your spouse. Your husband must please you too, but I'm talking to you right now. If you're going to have a fulfilling and joyful married life, you want to get a healthy attitude. I Corinthians 7:3 says your body does not belong to you, but to your spouse, and his body does not belong to him but to you. It is your job to find joy in pleasing your spouse. This is not just a want in a relationship but a need.

Your past issues may be lingering on in your mind. You may have been a bed missionary or wild. Either way, adjustments must be made to line up with the right design for a good marriage. Nobody says it's going to be easy, but it is worth it. Just like when you invest in a good pair of shoes. They may make your toes feel like they're balled up in a fist. But you know if you keep walking in them it'll get better. After about the fifth wearing, they are now your favorite shoes. You have to work out your marriage, finding that perfect way that turns you on.

It is well worth the time. Laughter is like medicine. When you finally get that perfect atmosphere in the bedroom that makes everything all right you will laugh all the way to work the next day.

Anything is possible if you believe. Sex *is* personal. No one can dictate to you how to enjoy your marital bed. It is a special moment of oneness between you and your spouse. If your time together is not like that, then there is an issue. This can be fixed but don't let your problems have anything to do with something holding onto wrong teaching. Sex has everything to do with how God formed the male and female bodies. It is perfect for enjoyable sex.

Of course, there can be an entire book on this subject. You can thank me later for the next chapter.

Let There Be Sex Part II

There can always be more to learn about sex and marriage. Nobody knows it all. There has been enough hypocritical rhetoric floating around to last three lifetimes. You may have heard it preached, your mama or daddy told you, or some staunchly religious person put their twist on how folks should operate in the bedroom. I'm not ashamed to say I'm open to learning anything else God wants me to know about sexual relations in a marriage. I take joy in learning all I can and sharing it with anyone who will listen. My goal is always to help as many people as I can. There is a myriad of information all across the globe. Just open up and know that even if it is good, it can be even better.

The Book of James in the Bible says it is joyful to have all kinds of temptations because it tests your faith. Your faith is only tested when you set your sights on a thing and want to see it manifest. That even counts for a goal of *not* doing certain things. You have to know what you believe to have faith in it. The principles contained in this book can give your marriage a completely new look if you apply them. Temptations are a part of everyone's life. Married folks are not exempt from being tempted. Your marriage should have an invisible clause that says, "I will do everything I can do to satisfy the desires of my spouse." Leaving it open to chance, your spouse may take a chance, and you will not like it. If I were you, I would not leave it open for the temptation to stand a chance in leading your spouse to cheat. Maybe you can resist it, but your spouse may not be as strong. You do not want to test their faith. There are enough temptations out there that will do that without you leaving them hanging.

You won't know what to do until you know, and you won't get there until you get there. But you will have to decide you want to do better and not continue living an unbalanced life that brings you grief in your marriage. Sex in a marriage is not the most time-consuming (tell the truth), but it is a powerful ten percent! Take it out of your relationship and see what you have left. Until you begin to miss something in your intimacy you won't know something is missing.

Tell yourself the truth—at times you are still haunted by things you did that you now regret. You are walking around like nothing is wrong, but it comes to the forefront of your mind every now and then. You must know there is an escape for every temptation, and you do not have to be held captive to every temptation. You may not have a clue on how to avoid the pitfalls that seem to follow you. There is wisdom concerning sex that is available to you, and you will never have to regret it again.

You will never *know* your spouse without sex. You want to stay in the know, then have more sex. God meant for couples to find pleasure in their marital bed. Since sex answers so many physical needs, it is good to discover the needs your spouse most desires to be met. Whether he/she is romantic or not, every human wants intimacy. Now some of you may stand back in ancient history with those who chose to be eunuchs (sexless) or you may have chosen the Catholic priesthood. But, for the rest of you, you need to stay in the know and keep your marriage whole.

There are several different ways to answer that natural desire for intimacy. Some days you just feel "in love" and want to demonstrate that love with sex. Sometimes it may be in the form of thanks for the happiness you feel. The final way is when you both need a good screw. Yes, I said it! It doesn't matter all the turmoil of the day; a good screw can answer your heart. Not only have you both satisfied that natural desire for intimacy, but you have also healed some physical ailments.

Before I get into the benefits to your body that sex provides, I want to put out a disclaimer. God did not make mistakes. Singles can decide to stay single and live long, productive lives. As scripture tells us in II Corinthians 7, singles have more opportunity for ministry than married folks do. God put health benefits in many things. The disclaimer is this: I am not advocating that singles use the health benefits of sex to start or continue sinning. Until marriage, they can find many ways to stay healthy! Keep your body healthy, and then when you are married you can add the other benefits that sex gives.

On the website Newvision.co.ug there is an article about the health benefits of sex. It is worth it to discuss a few of them here:

- During sex, there is a release of something called oxytocin. Oxytocin is a natural painkiller. Sex, in this case, may reduce or alleviate some body aches and pains.
- Oxytocin is a hormone and it also is in your body to assist in trust and bonding. Since it is released during sex it plays a big part in the connectivity that happens during sex.
- Sex is a direct result of lower blood pressure. Joseph J. Pinzone, medical director of Amai Wellness does says "Research suggests a link between sex and lower blood pressure."
- It is an antidote for longer life, and this is due to the good heart rate sex could afford you. England Research Institute has proposed that men who indulge in frequent sex are less likely to have heart diseases.
- Good sex could equal good life. This is a result of a healthy heart from frequent sex.
- From all the good mood hormones that flood your system during sex, depression and anxiety are overcome.

- The release of dopamine during sex helps reduce the stress that has built up during the day and thereby aids in a night of good sleep.
- Builds your immunity. More sex helps maintain the release of Immunoglobulin A, an antigen that helps protect the body from disease.
- A study suggests that sex reduces the chances of getting prostate cancer in men.

There are about eight more listed on this site. If you research the subject, you can probably find more than that. Read the article for yourself: https://www.newvision.co.ug/news/1463477/health-benefits-regular-sex.

Not only is sex good for your health, but if everything comes before your sex life, everything else is dying. Sex is what makes a marriage a marriage. There is a spiritual connection that happens in the act of intercourse. You are growing further and further apart if you are in a sexless marriage. The bad part is if you are denying your spouse sex, you are also cheating yourself. Sex is an exchange of energy that each partner needs. A poor sex life is less quality of life. Studies show that married people are generally healthier. Now, I am not going to blow it out of proportion. Diet and exercise play a big part in the health of all humans, but marriage adds even more benefits to this fact. Don't take away from these benefits by killing what's thriving by not having sex.

Sex is what makes a marriage a marriage

Maybe it sounds exciting for single men and women to discuss their sexual prowess with each other. That may be exciting, but as a marriage age, finding new ways to please your spouse is a plus. It is unrealistic to believe a high sex drive will last forever. Read the studies. It is better to know you may find yourself too busy in life to think of sex as a priority. The best way is to make it an important attribute to keeping a marriage vibrant.

Unless you have done the research, you may not know that vibrators were created in the 1800s to relieve something called "female hysteria." Women were coming into doctor's offices with everything from depression to anxiety. The doctors would perform pelvic massages and the patients would be instantly healed. Now you may think the doctors would be enjoying this therapy, but sometimes the service would take up to an hour. Doctors began to complain about sore hands. Dr. Joseph Mortimer Granville came up with the first help for the symptom. It was initially called a manipulator (https://www.huffingtonpost.com.au2016/08/18/the-vibrators-long-fascinating-history-of-discovery-and-rsi_a_21454596/#:~:text=Vibrators). Now, do you think women are any different in physicality than they were in the 1800s? "Female hysteria" still exists, but you may know it as PMS accompanied by bloating. Orgasms are still the cure for "female hysteria."

Although married couples enjoy each other's bodies, each participant needs to be selfish. Once you work on "getting yours" you will be more inclined to make sure your spouse is getting his/hers too. Satisfied people are more inclined to satisfy. The key is to practice getting pleased and pleasing all at the same time!

Sex is a healer. It opens up couples in ways that plain communication cannot. Don't get me wrong, communication is very important, but sex speaks volumes between two people who are in love. If you still have that "hold back" attitude because of what you were taught about sex, get rid of it. Sex is glorious and can heal where other things cannot.

The emotional connection with your spouse cannot even be explained to those who have not regularly experienced it. If you have been starved in this area, it is never too late for some training. Seek out a sex therapist, find books, look it up online. Do not let another day go by where you feel helpless in this area. The emotional connection is established by including passion, spirituality, and intimacy.

You want to find a really good time, find that place, arena, or atmosphere that gets your sexy going. No one can tell you where your most comfortable "bed" is. It could be in the shower. Maybe it is in the ocean. I cannot state all the possible times or places; you just have to discover yours. After a nice dinner date or movie, or sneaking after the kids are asleep. Wherever you find it, repeat it often. Screw just to have a good time.

The marriage bed is undefiled (Hebrews 13:4). When did we start to get rules in the bedroom? It is the advent of the rules created by religious mindsets that have opened up confusion about the bed in marriage. The bed represents the unified place where couples lie together. Keeping the marriage bed pure leaves room for the openness and privacy shared intimately by a couple. The purity opens up the opportunities to explore each other's bodies and finding comfort and erogeneity in the arms of your lover. In this place, there is no comparing of other partners, no traveling of thoughts to other sexual encounters, and only the intimacy found between the couple enjoying each other's sexual relations. The way to keep the bed undefiled is to continue to explore ways to satisfy your spouse and not allow the interference of past taught prejudices about sex. Undefiled is the absence of anyone else's opinions or other experiences that have no right to how you and your spouse enjoy your bed.

The best way to guarantee a good sex life is to know what you like. Your erogenous zone may be on your shoulder. You will not know this unless it is discovered. Never be ashamed to speak up. If your back is being rubbed and that's not it, speak up. If you plan to stay married, your words or actions will mean the most in the importance of your sexual relations. Discover your body and be better equipped to direct your spouse on how to please you in the bed.

Keeping the bed undefiled starts with how you conduct yourself when you're not in the bed. This is where God comes in. Establishing a close relationship with God can guard against all those close encounters that you run to avoid. It could have started with a little flirting at work. Then it moved to an innocent lunch. The next thing you know, you are hot and bothered or maybe in a compromising position that you have no clue how to get out of. If this happened already, ask God's forgiveness and then forgive yourself. God knew you would be tempted, but there is always a way to get out. You do not have to live thinking it is all up to how much you can control yourself. Know your weakness so that your marriage will not suffer unnecessarily. What you do outside has a way of following you home. You will not always be at home. Prepare yourself by keeping your relationship with God intact so that He can give you the warning signs that could defile what you are working so hard to establish.

Your mind is where the good, bad, and ugly start. Tame your thought life. Finding ways to please your spouse is your first line of defense. Men have emotions, but God fixed it so that their bodies' makeup puts them more in charge during the act of having sex. God does not want man or woman to cheat, but women cheating have more negative ramifications than men cheating. To God, it doesn't matter whether it's a man or a woman; He is not pleased. If you are a woman reading this, please listen closely. Men have the hardest time forgiving women who cheat. If you want to think about it technically, then pay attention here. A man has an appendage he puts inside a woman. The woman is receiving something from a man. Many men cannot fathom this happening to his wife. I say all this so that all you believers can work on your thought life. Keep your mind, and it gives you more power over your body. Do not let it get started; bring all of your thoughts into compliance with what God says.

Saying "let there be sex" implies more from your bed. As you interact with people outside of your home there will always be an opportunity for someone to see what your spouse has. Being married will not stop some undisciplined adult from trying to get you into their bed. Keep yourself from the danger of the inability to resist temptation. Make sure you are getting plenty at home, which in turn will leave no room for any extras. The way to block this is simple. The Bible is clear. It does not say to pray. It does not say to get counseling. You know what it says: "Run!" I Corinthians 6:18 actually says to "flee fornication." This is the same recommendation for adultery. You want to know how to do this, do not compromise your integrity. You want more sex, get it at home.

You may be single and most likely not a virgin, but it is never too late to make a fresh start. Stop putting yourself in situations you have little strength to get out of. Stop providing ways for your flesh to fail you, and begin to build your spirit with a good, durable relationship with God. The issue is past experience. As mentioned earlier, singles have more time for ministry. Do not let your extra time be spent finding ways to mess with your destiny. Start from today and get a fresh start.

There's nothing like telling your flesh, "No!" and meaning it. You will find enough grace to take you further than you could have ever gotten alone. But you have to believe this for it to work. God's grace is sufficient for you because His grace is made perfect when you are weak (II Corinthians 12:9). This is the whole reason why God sent Jesus and ultimately the Holy Spirit to help you when you need Him.

Contrary to what you may have been told, if you are not married, you will not explode if you are not currently having sex. This "let there be sex" is for when it should be. You can get past those nights of longing. You'll be okay.

Sex in marriage is to establish the oneness that God designed. You have to live in the intrigue of becoming one. In the last chapter, I discussed the physical act of making love, but there is a spiritual part. You cannot become one unless you understand the spiritual part of sex.

Sex brings you together in more than one way. The consummation of marriage is a meeting of the minds and hearts. It brings you into a oneness that cannot be attained without sex. This act does the same thing every time it is performed. That is why sex should be a regular part of your union.

Making excuses not to is wrong. If you want to help seal your marriage from adultery, let there be sex and let it be consistent. Sex has healing virtues. It is a spirit fixer. It caps apologies after a fight like nothing else can. It reestablishes the union when you have been apart for legitimate reasons.

Apply the sexual principles to your marriage that will ensure it brings you together during some of the most difficult situations. Even when you don't feel like it, do it. When you do that, make sure your man or woman has no idea you're faking. There's no worse bruising to a man's ego than sex performed by a wife who acts like she's dreading every minute and can't wait until you're finished. It has to be worse for a woman because she's built to be in touch with her emotions. Men, if your love and passion are directed at your wife, then faking will never be a part. Coming together often brings healing and peace to any situation.

Sex is not a cure-all but it is the next best thing. It can answer for many things that otherwise will remain aggravating. Sex as dessert after a hard day, sneaking sex after the kids are asleep, sex after a night out, etc., are all ways to enhance and add romance to your marriage. Let there be sex, and let there be plenty of it!

Forget all that you may have heard before. Start from what you're hearing today. Just like the new traditions you may establish in your own house with your own family, start some traditions in your bed with your spouse. Sex can take on a life of its own if you will allow it to. What you heard in the past may have silenced the creativity of two bodies owned by two people in love with each other.

Looks Part I

You've had three babies and look nothing like you did when you walked down the aisle. Your stretch marks draw a road map from New York to California, and Mount Rushmore separates your abdomen from your chest. Now he's complaining. He wants his wife back, and you're mad. You're tired of the nagging about your eating habits and body size. The problem is that you don't think it's fair.

Your self-esteem has collapsed to the floor, and you see no way out except in divorce court. Before you make that decision final, I want you to look at some things that maybe you haven't thought of before.

First, I want to examine some unrealistic expectations that have plagued us all. The media is the first defendant. Most of what's shown in the media are fake. Photoshopped and airbrushed; you have been played. You are comparing yourself to a façade. Her abs aren't real and neither is her backside. But you are depressed because you know you can never stand up to those looks.

Who said that 36-24-36 are the winning numbers? Who made up those measurements? Confucius, the Chinese philosopher (among other things) once said, "Everything has beauty; not everyone sees it" (www.Goodreads.com). This statement tells me anything can be beautiful to the person who embraces it.

"He has made everything beautiful in its time" (Eccl. 3:11). So, everything created has a time for its beauty to be revealed. When is that time? The moment you decide to accept what you have to offer.

The pain from an insult is a result of how you feel about it. If you think your abs are ugly, then don't wait for your husband to say it. Do something about it. The pain in his words comes from their connection to what you have already told yourself, but maybe not out loud.

If you have a Ph.D. and a high school dropout calls you stupid, would that bother you? Most likely not because you made some sacrifices to get an education and you do not have any relation to what it feels like to not finish high school. That should be the same way you handle poor body image. You can do something about it.

First off, it is a psychological fact that no one can change another person (www.Psychcentral.com). With that in mind, it makes sense to decide you will do better and not try to act on being better because you are being criticized. If you lose fifty pounds to please your husband or boyfriend, you most likely will put it back on and add a few more pounds to go with it. You have to do it because *you* want to. You must work on the inside, and it will manifest on the outside.

Looks have played a part ever since the beginning of time. In the Old Testament of the Bible, David the King watched a beautiful married woman, Bathsheba, take a bath. He summoned her over to his place and lays with her (had sex!). She becomes pregnant. After several failed concocted schemes to cover his mess he plots to have her husband, Uriah, placed on the front lines of war where he is killed. Then he marries her. What was the attraction? Her beauty that he could not resist (II Samuel 11).

Way before this happens, Samuel is sent to pick a king for Israel from the house of Jesse, who has eight sons. Samuel goes through each son, based on their looks, exclaiming, "He must be the one!" After seeing seven sons he asks Jesse if there is anyone else. Jesse cannot believe a king could not be chosen from any of the seven "fine" sons Samuel had a chance to look over. He calls out to the ruddy shepherd boy of a son, who is out in the field with the stinky sheep. Of course, he turns out to be the one. This is the same son who connives to take another's wife, David (I Samuel 16).

Isn't it ironic he wasn't the best-looking son, but he ends up with one of the finest women? What happened? David developed his swag from the inside. Of course, being king gave him some credentials. But, he did not lack confidence. I want you to tap into what's on the inside of you. God did not make a mess when He made you. You just have to find that beauty that belongs to you.

You do all kinds of things to make yourself look good. But what are you basing your beauty on? Are you looking at the photoshopped and airbrushed covers of the magazines? Are you basing beauty on reality television shows? You can be inspired by these things but be you. Your beauty has to come from within you. It's already there, but you have to find it. Learn and be inspired but be you.

Your swag comes from the inside. It has nothing to do with how you look. You have to tap into your swag to make it work. I have seen too many women who get divorced and then decide to make a change for the better in their appearance. Why couldn't they do that while they were married? The beauty inside is what fosters the beauty that shows up on the outside.

I believe it's an insult to the marriage that someone would decide to get motivated after divorcing. How do you know getting you together will not change the entire atmosphere of the union? Think about the health benefits and the emotional. Plus, it will be when working out and eating right is part of your daily routine. You'll look in the mirror and exclaim, "Is that really me?" This can only happen when you decide you are beautiful and worth the time. Make that change before even discussing divorce. Why wait until your issues with self-esteem and lack of care in the looks department add to other life concerns forcing divorce to be put on the table? Apologize to yourself and make that change.

If you do all you can and divorce still happens, you will not live with regrets. You should not get yourself together just to please your man; you should do it for yourself. You are taking care of yourself for yourself. You are not good to anybody out of shape and feeling like a mess. Get yourself together for yourself, and then you will start feeling better. And if the marriage ends, you know you did all you could and gave 100% of yourself. Successful marriages are when both people give 100%. This kind of marriage does not end in divorce. Make your insides beautiful, and you will not be able to keep it from the outside.

Beauty is based on grace and charm like the subtle hues of blue you may see in a gallery painting. It's the magnet that draws you to a person. You may be single and waiting to meet the right person, but you are not right yet. You have to get *yourself* right first. He is not going to make you right; *you* have to make you right. You have to decide for yourself where your beauty is. If you discover your beauty and embrace it, it won't be hard for others to see it also.

"You are fearfully and wonderfully made," is what David wrote in Psalms. He understood each person is unique. Like a snowflake, no two are alike. Everything that looks perfect is not perfect. There are too many beautiful people walking around who are seemingly gorgeous on the outside but have jacked-up insides. That's why your beauty has to start from the inside first. Know in advance you are beautiful before you start upgrading yourself (exercising, new hairdo, makeup, etc.).

Make your beauty the "it" thing. If you want to attract anybody, you have to have yourself together.

So the question is: are looks important for a relationship?

My answer is yes.

You won't get the chance to display your inner beauty if the outside looks like a mess. If you are single, you need to stop leaving the house with hair rollers and pajama bottoms on (carrying a pillow!). What's the purpose of going to the grocery store before you brush your teeth, looking like you just woke up and it is two p.m.?

Look like what you're trying to bring into your life. I do not want to imagine what kind of person would desire a woman who walks around in the mall with bedroom slippers on, a rag on her head, and crust in her eyes. If I cannot imagine that, I am sure this is not the kind of person you want to attract.

Do good looks make a good marriage? This is a weighted question. You may have been initially attracted to each other because you look good, but is that enough to keep a marriage together?

You have to go deeper. He was a hunk of a man, all chiseled up. You compared him to Idris Elba before long days at the office and the stress of a new home took their toll. Now, his six-pack is a fat pack, and his hair is half there and half gone. Are you going to nag him every day or run and leave him because he won't change? There is more to him than his body.

Love in a marriage must go deeper than what meets the eye. You want the love that lasts, you have to go deeper. The shallow end does not yield much of a catch. Start fishing the day you get married. You will find more than what you expected. Deep things call to deep things. His six-pack and ripped-up triceps cannot pay the car note.

As you age, things, needs, and love change. You may want to stop comparing what you have to what is not in your house. That fantasy that you're comparing your spouse to does not love you like that and will not meet your needs. As the years add up reassess what you really want and adjust your mindset away from the superficial things of immature new beginnings. There is a way to find that joyful place that outlasts being a diva.

Looks matter but not enough to be grounds to run the other way. If you married simply for looks, then you have to find that common ground that attracted you on a deeper level. Maybe it was his intelligence. He intrigued you with his well-rounded conversation. If that is the case then add some variety to your interests. Hang with a more intelligent crowd, go to a museum on the weekend, or read some books that will give you other things to talk about.

This chapter has only scratched the surface. Part II of Looks will complete the dish on looks and relationships.

Looks Part II

I have already tapped the surface about your inner swag. You may have tried all kinds of ways to pump up your self-esteem. You did self-talk, read books on positive reinforcement, and collected all the pamphlets on the habits of successful people. Nothing, so far, has seemed to work. I have a guaranteed answer if you are willing to put down all your prior efforts and listen to the real truth. Your maker, God, knows you more than you know yourself, and He made you fearful and wonderful.

God made you so that He could live in you and direct your efforts to run this world. With this in mind, what are you giving Him to live in? You want to know how to conquer the world, but you have not asked or learned how to take control of your own body.

I told you in the last chapter that looks count, but they aren't all there is. In this chapter, I want to give you the rest of my thoughts on this matter. If you do not like the way you look, do something about it. You are already beautiful to your creator, but you have the power in you to fix what you do not like and to forget about the rest. Why dwell on the long scar on your arm when you can have perfect abs?

You can't want tight quadriceps to look like an Olympic track star just because you saw her on the cover of *Muscle* magazine. But you can want it because working out will help you live a more healthy and productive life. Why should you work to tone your body? It's healthier for your heart and other organs.

It is estimated that somewhere in the neighborhood of $190.2 billion is spent on healthcare, or 21% of medical care is spent on obesity-related illnesses in the United States (www.healthycommunitieshealthyfuture.org). Why not be a part of the solution? That is if you want to. Nobody is going to force you, but it is something you may want to consider.

You should not get healthier to get a man, and you can't do it to keep a man, but you can do it for yourself and God. This can only be embraced with higher-level thinking. Even if you grew up eating five pieces of bacon and two bowls of grits every morning, who said you have to keep on eating like that? I call this kind of teaching selfish righteousness. You decide to do it right because it is right, not because your mama, friends, lovers, or man said so. You want to please your Maker and you want to feel better about yourself.

You have to first take hold of the truth that you are beautiful just like you are now and the rules on what looks the best are manmade. Who said washboard abs are the best way, or that women with hair down their backs are better looking? You do not have to believe the hype. You know what category you are in. Choose what is best for you and go for it. You decide!

Fragmented people do things based on what other people say. They're constantly looking to others for affirmation. These people have an issue with everything. They are never satisfied. Even great compliments from their spouse do nothing to build them up. They find themselves in a cycle of never finding that happy place; they want affirmation, but the words never seem to hit home. If this is you, it can be changed. You have to start from the inside. It's an internal job. If you do not grip your beauty, then even doing something about it will not help you.

You may be trying to hold onto your spouse, but you are constantly putting yourself down. The roll on your back that he thinks is cute suddenly becomes more and more hideous every time you complain about its ugliness. Some men love their lady's looks and have not noticed the fine woman crossing the street until you and your insecurities point out her beauty. "Look at that girl. She thinks her hair is on point!" He hadn't noticed until you showed him where to look. Now he's checking out her firm legs, flowing hair, and tight dress. You can't get mad because you're beautiful too but don't know it, and if you hadn't opened your mouth the woman would have simply crossed the street!

You have to stop being intimidated by other people who you think have something more than you. Who told you they did? Back in the Old Testament of the Bible, twelve spies went out to see how to take over some land. Two came back telling the leader they could win the battle and ten came back saying there are giants in the land and they were but grasshoppers (Numbers 13). Your intimidation comes from inside you. A bully is only a bully to those who think he is. (The two positive spies were right. The whole crew went and conquered the land!)

You have to love how you are made. It is your look. It is yours exclusively. It is time for you to accept the gift God has given you in your makeup. It is solely yours. There is no one made just like you. You have to become whole in this knowledge.

I have six points to direct you to your wholeness. You start working on them and watch the change take place.

6 Points to Direct you to Your Wholeness

1. **Get rid of anything stunting your growth.**

   If you are constantly around complaining people, cut them off. You are trying to get somewhere, and they are setting you back every time they open their mouths.

2. **Do not listen to anyone who does not have an investment in your future.**

   If your spouse wants you to stop cooking chitterlings, do not listen to your "friend" who says you grew up on them and you do not have to listen to him. She most likely does not have a spouse, is on her fifth spouse, or the one she has is on his way out the door.

3. **Start believing the positive feedback of your companion.**

If you constantly hear how beautiful you are, accept it. If you do not believe it, say thank you and smile then work on yourself until you know you are really beautiful. Begin to work on the changeable things you feel make you less attractive.

4. **You will be on the right road to wholeness when you admit the truth to yourself.**

If you know you need to get your hair done then do that. You do not have to wait to see how it compares to other folks' hair or when your spouse starts to complain. If you need to get your teeth cleaned, do that. You can see the yellow yourself when you brush them. There is no sense in starting a full-blown fight when you are insulted about a truth. You knew it before he said it!

5. **Forget about those things that you cannot change and work on those things that can be changed.**

You are not able to shrink your feet, but you can get a pedicure or go to the dollar store and buy a toenail clip and some colorful polish.

6. **No more excuses!**

Y'all Just Need a Remix

You've heard of a remix. You know when you have heard a song on the radio that sounds similar to an old song? That is because the song has been reintroduced with some current nuances that will appeal to an old and new audience. This is what I am saying some couples need. Remix is not brand new, it's a reconstitution of what already exists. Do you want something new? Then take what you have and remix it. When it's finished it has a brand-new flavor. Some things may have to go, while some things, in love, just need to be remixed.

One thing you must know about a love relationship is that both parties must agree on any grand change that's going to take place. If your spouse does not want to go out with you, going out stag will not answer the problem. A compromise is the only way to make a relationship last forever. You have to have a meeting of the minds. I want to mention a Scripture here, not to start preaching, but to explain what it means to remix your love affair. You both must agree that something is going to change.

What's really going on in your love life? I'm not just talking about sex; I'm talking about the entire relationship. If from the beginning you discussed making your relationship last, then remixing will be a natural part of what happens. If that discussion never took place, then you have to agree to talk about it. I am going to tell you one thing if you're unhappy, your partner is also unhappy. There's no way to be in a beautiful, loving marriage and one person is totally dissatisfied, unfulfilled, and unhappy. A marriage takes two. You cannot be in a relationship with yourself. Find out what's going on in your house. You have to ask the right questions. Is your spouse really satisfied, or are you both hanging onto the idea of marriage with little contentment?

When you took your vows, if you did not decide you would stay together for the rest of your lives, maybe a discussion can happen now. Just because the preacher or the justice of the peace at the courthouse quoted the traditional vows, "in sickness and health, for better or worse and till death do you part," and you answered "I do," that does not necessarily mean you will. The proof of this is in the divorce rate and the remarriage rate. Today it is not surprising to hear someone in their forties say they have been married three times. It's not even usual for a twenty-five-year-old to say they have three kids and they're already divorced. So revisiting the original vows is a thought. You are not trying to guilt someone into going back to visit something they said just to make them comply. The thought is to reconsider what you can do to make things better and possibly make the marriage last a lifetime.

I am a firm believer in marriage counseling. Actually, I'm a firm believer in all kinds of counseling. But for this writing, I'm talking about marriage counseling or sex counseling, anything that will make your marriage better. But you don't have to go to counseling. The point of all of this is that you have to have a meeting of the minds. The Scripture I want to insert is: "Can two walk together, except they be agreed?" (Amos 3:3) Do you know what this means? Many have taught these words to mean you cannot stay in the company of someone with whom you do not agree. If you do a study on this passage you'll find it means two people must agree to have a discussion. That's the point of this remix chapter. Do the work of a counselor even if you don't pay someone to do the work for which they have a degree. If you can peacefully discuss your differences, do that. But if extra help is needed, there is always counseling,

If you both decide you want this relationship to work, then you both can agree to do some remixing. If you were in the music industry you would find that if you liked an old song and wanted to use it in a new song the writer of the song would have to agree to let you do that. And for a sum of money, you could borrow this song to remix into something new. You understand now that any change in a relationship must first be discussed and agreed upon by both parties.

Remix it, baby. Let's take that dull interaction and add some bling and make it new again. Both of you will find a new fan in your spouse. Do you remember the chapter on the happiness test? This is an upgrade. Remix. Don't just do the same old things trying to make your spouse happy. Add some spice. And please do not ignore the cries for change. Maybe the bedroom needs some more heat. Maybe you start caring more about how you look. This goes for men and women. Are you all doing the same old boring things day after day, week after week, month after month, year after year? What about a vacation to an exotic location? Yes, that's what I said—remix it.

Do not decide by yourself how a remix will take place. Agree to walk together and discuss what you both want. Compromising is what I'm talking about. Remember, you can't be happy by yourself in a relationship if you're calling it a relationship. Your job is to be happy and share that happiness with your spouse. You can be happy by yourself, but if you're not trying to make your spouse happy, you'll be by yourself. No one is responsible for another person's happiness, but your job as a spouse is to do the little things that will bring happiness to your spouse. This may sound like an oxymoron, but it's all about relationships. When you give happiness and contentment to someone else, it is returned to you. Years pass by and what you used to like may not be what you like now. You can't play a song from 1982 in 2020 and think it's going to be a real number one hit. This is no different in a relationship. Things get old. You have to spice it up; go off the map to make things great again.

Happiness flows in cycles. It may have been funny ten years ago, but it's not fun anymore. Even clothes and styles come back every twenty years and then leave again. I guarantee those relationships lasting for fifty years aren't going through the same drama the same way. Those couples found a way to cycle that happiness. Even some bad habits can take on a more tolerable form. Maybe you still don't wash clothes, but those drawers find their way into the hamper. Maybe that head rag is now a silk scarf embellished with small rhinestones. Catch your cycle and make it happen.

The two of you can determine when it's time for a remix. Or maybe you can do a surprise remix. Sometimes it may be time for one person's remix and the other person has to catch up. Either way, it will be beneficial for both of you.

Tips for Remixing your relationship:

- **Sexual Remix**
    - Attend Sexual Counseling for ideas and ways to improve your sex
- **Physical Remix**
    - Workout together and/or on your own
- **Emotional Remix**
    - Go to therapy- talk to someone about what you are feeling and learn ways to deal with your issues, your past, and your emotions
- **Spiritual Remix**
    - Spend time with God (prayer, fasting, scripture reading, meditating)
- **Dream Remix**

Attend workshops, events, and conferences to spike your dreams

This Turns Me On

She keeps rubbing my feet. She might have a foot fetish. I'm not sure, but the nerves on the bottom of my feet are very sensitive. Her rubbing is not very comfortable. I really don't like it, but she's completely into it. Sometimes I look down at her and her eyes are closed as she oils and lets her fingers glide between my toes. My feet are not an erogenous zone for me.

No, this is not the story of my life, but I'm sure it rings true with somebody. This chapter is not even about sexual arousal, although it is about where it starts. Sexual intercourse, or whatever you want to call it, does not always start between the sheets. If you ask a woman she say might say it starts in the morning. But as quiet as it is kept, men like some other types of foreplay that have nothing to do with making physical love.

Can you tell your spouse what turns you on? That's really not the question. Of course, you can tell your spouse anything you want. The point is to be able to express whatever it is that turns you on and not feel that retribution will come. Turning you on is a big part of a lasting relationship. You should be able to express yourself freely.

If you like little or big gifts but your spouse just wants to spend every moment of the day cuddling, that may be a problem. No, there's nothing wrong with warm embraces but if that's the only thing your spouse thinks turns you on and you know there are other things, you must speak up. The saying "closed mouths don't get fed" is not about begging for food so you don't starve. Your spouse has to be taught how to meet your emotional needs. They may be trying. Before you shut the book because you think I'm talking about women serving men, think again. The meeting of needs goes both ways. He may think he's pleasing you, but he keeps buying you flowers when what you actually like is to watch him frying you some French fries.

I've heard "happy wife means a happy life." Have you ever heard the saying, "a happy man means the house will stand"? This is so true. Okay, I just made that up, but both spouses need their egos stroked. Talk it out. It may sting at first if your spouse thinks you've always been happy with what they perceived was a show of affection. But you can only fake happiness for so long. Make-believe happy is just that—make-believe. The house will never be happy if one spouse is not. It takes two.

> **The house will never be happy if one spouse is not**

If you do not want him to buy flowers for you, he can take you out twice a month if that's what you want. You don't think he will? Did you ask? Does he know how you feel? Have a heart to heart and not right after he comes in the house with two dozen long-stem roses. Wrong time! Two Saturdays after the roses have drooped, and you both are lying in bed watching cartoons, maybe then you can say, "Hey, bae, I want to ask you something."

"What do you need, bae?" he might ask.

You say, "I appreciate you spending so much money on all those beautiful flowers for me. Do you think we can go out once in a while, maybe once or twice a month? I really would like that along with all the nice things you do for me."

If you say it in a calm and gentle tone of voice you may get an excellent response. You can even surprise him with the outing that you plan. You know your spouse and hopefully have learned how he likes to communicate. The tone of voice and attitude is a love language of its own.

Every ounce of your interaction makes a difference in your relationship. Practice the art of being assertive. Your happiness and contentment are part of the whole package. If you do not take care of yourself, you will never know how to properly please your spouse. Love flows from the inside out. You get your measure of emotional needs met, and you will be equipped to give back the same.

No one can help how they are made. If he would rather have time with you rather than a new pair of Js, are you going to preach to him how much you spent on them Js? All he wants is you in the house for a few hours keeping him company. She may love when you help her fold the towels, but you keep lying in the bed butt naked like that's going to solve all problems. It's okay if both of your sweet spots are totally different. The name of the game is compromise.

If she won't say what she likes, if he refuses to complain about anything you do, then watch his reaction to the things you do. You both can learn what the other enjoys by more than one method. It can be accomplished through trial and error or a few pleasant conversations.

Stop tolerating those acts of kindness if you aren't happy with them and learn how to ask for what you would rather have. Happiness is contagious. Ask for what would turn you on and allow your spouse to do the same even if it hurts a little because you thought you were doing a good job.

When both needs are met, it's great for the entire family. People can tell when something's not right in the Kool-Aid. Talk about your love languages. That's making love already.

Intellectual Masturbation
(Getting to know you)

Being alone is underrated. Most people go out into the world and hope they can meet other people who will like them. What's funny is when they don't connect as they imagine, they will turn the discomfort outward, blaming the new people they're meeting. Most never stop to think that it's an inside job. Being alone and being honest with yourself will solve this problem.

When you're alone, you will discover many of the things that frustrate you. Always being around people and running your mouth only strengthens your insecurities and character flaws. You then find fault with other people, not knowing that what's aggravating you about them are the same things you see in yourself, but it's now reflected in them. Being with yourself will point out these things. Once you are aware of your faults you can begin correcting them. Upgrading who you are builds a love affair with yourself. When you go out into the world and someone points out a flaw, you won't get angry. You can just say, "Thank you. I'm working on that." I know that's not a normal response, but it can be if you are willing to work on yourself by yourself. There's no sense in suppressing the things that frustrate you when you're alone; that's the opportunity to work on them without comments from the outside world.

It is hard to get other people to like you when you don't like yourself. Here you are begging for love, and you don't know how to love yourself, forget about *liking* yourself! Learning to love yourself takes time. The majority of that time will be when you are alone. I was talking to a therapist about the best way to ensure better love relationships. Her answer surprised me. She said women need to explore their bodies to present their whole selves to their love interest. How can a woman hate something about her life, her body, or her experiences and then be comfortable bringing all this with her into her next relationship?

This is an awkward subject to talk about, but it shouldn't be. After all, it is your own body and what your whole self has been through is what makes you, you. Who better to know about it than you? This same sentiment is the idea of men knowing themselves intellectually. Men don't know themselves emotionally; that is why when women ask them hard questions they feel violated. Stimulating yourself intellectually will lead to emotional

> **Stimulating yourself intellectually will lead to emotional breakthroughs**

breakthroughs. When you are honest with yourself about where you are in life and where you want to go, it won't be hard to share this with all the people once you have embraced it yourself. The term for this activity is "intellectual masturbation." That is because it starts alone, but it doesn't stay there. It is very hard to keep exciting revelations to yourself, whether they are good, bad, or indifferent. This time alone is when you begin to really like yourself.

Before I receive any flack because of what I said about women exploring their bodies, let me add that it's a known fact that men already doing it. You don't hear much publicly about women practicing the same. Many do, but it is just not talked about. Intellectual masturbation is more than sexual arousal; it is learning the ins and outs of yourself so your partner does not have to guess. It is also to benefit you. It is about loving all of you. When you embrace every part of your being no one can have control over any part of you but God. What is wrong with loving every inch of your body and then discovering the strengths of your psyche? I don't care what anyone says, everything about you is yours to own. Yes, this book is addressing women, but I have not left men out of the equation. Alone with intellectual masturbation is for everyone.

When you get by yourself and run into that area you hate about you, be open about it. Shut that imaginary audience out. There is only you and God. If you have kids, send them away sometimes, if only for a few hours. One good day to start is the next time you blow up about something seemingly insignificant. It may seem very serious at the moment of impact, but your alone time can sift through the drama. Loving yourself like God loves you can silence any critique.

You can see why being alone is very important. It's not a subject that is talked about very much. You can find hundreds of books on love relationships and various friendships but learning to love yourself by yourself is rarely spoken about. Researchers are starting to develop information concerning this subject. Even introverts are being discussed as not wanting to be alone all the time or finding joy in time with themselves and also doing social activities (https://www.verywellmind.com/the-benefits-of-being-by-yourself-4769939). This is because there's a big difference between being alone and loneliness. Being alone is a choice, and loneliness is isolation from others for reasons other than your choosing. Know the difference and benefit from alone time.

If you find yourself alone and lonely, it may be beneficial to find out why. Find time for outside relationships and a newfound relationship with yourself being alone. If you do this you will find social gatherings will be that much more fulfilling. Understand the difference between alone and loneliness and choose alone often enough to build yourself up. I guarantee you will be a much better company when you do this.

So many people immediately find advocates when relationships explode in their faces. This may be good comfort at the time, but who are you talking to that can tell you where you did anything wrong? Polonius is a character in William Shakespeare's play

Hamlet. One of the most famous lines of the play was spoken by him: "To thine own self be true." Why would you lie to yourself? Yet that's what you do every time you are hurt, and nothing is ever your fault. That kind of sentiment is neither intellectual nor freeing. A bad breakup does not always mean that one person was at fault. While you are freshly dealing with the trauma may not be the time when you can point a finger at yourself, but at some point taking responsibility for your part is the best medicine.

If you spend every waking moment outside of work with your significant other, you may never discover why certain things bother you. I recommend counseling, mentoring, and time with you to practice information with yourself without interference from friends, well-wishers, and those people who seem to know it all. Know yourself to the fullest and every area of your romantic relationship will get better.

This is not textbook stuff for me. This is straight from my personal experience. I had to learn to do this myself, and I'm so glad I did. I am much better for it. Learning to love you is not spoken enough about. Receive the message, practice the concepts, spread it so others can enjoy being alone, and then share your new upgraded self with others.

When you have spent enough time with you, what you present to others is more than enough. Do not be one who jumps from one bad relationship into the next or the wife who constantly criticizes her husband because her own faults blind her to her truth. When you have been alone enough times you will find comfort in it. You will love romance, but there is nothing better than the love relationship between you and God. Recall that Mark 12:31 tells you to love you first so you know how to love others, not the other way around. Explore the beauty in all that you are—your mind (spirit), your soul, and your body. Present to others the relationship that you and God built.

Intellectual Masturbation Process:

1. **Alone Time**
   o Stimulate your brain
   o Enjoy yourself
   o Learn new things about you
   o Rediscover yourself

2. **Share the new you**
   o Upgrade you (new wardrobe, new hairdo, new attitude, exercise)
   o Attend social events
   o Share yourself in levels

Self-Love is the Best love

I'm not sure where the idea came from to give out all the love you could and hope and pray that it gets returned. It's not a biblical principle or a tenet practiced in any faith I have ever read or heard about. Still, it is a rule many practices to their detriment. Seems to me it came out of desperation.

According to New Testament teachings, believers have two great commandments that cover everything and anything they will face in this world. The commandments are to love God with everything that is in you and to love others as you love yourself. How can you practice loving others if you do not know how to love yourself? Then there is the fact that you have no clue about love unless you learn how to love *love*. That means putting all your energy and adoration into God because He is love. It is also understanding the love of God. These are the principles that will answer the call of your heart. God made them commands to free everyone who will practice them.

> **You will not love yourself correctly if you don't love God first**

You will not love yourself correctly if you don't love God first. Not only did He love you first, but He created love. Can you imagine switching seats in a car with an eight-month-old baby? What does a baby know about driving? He just started holding his own bottle. He is attached to his mommy because she feeds him, bathes him, and keeps his room temperature regulated. He has to mature in all he is learning. He must grow, then learn how to read, take a test, then be taught how to drive. This is the same set of principles you need to learn with God as your Father. You must cling to Him because He wants to nurture you. Come to Him as a baby does to his mother. He will show you how to eat; He will clean you up; He will give you the right temperature and atmosphere for you to grow, and then you can learn how He operates and win for yourself. Follow God's principles first and let them overflow in your life. After this is done you will know how to share them with others as God has shared them with you.

If you love God first and then turn that same energy towards yourself (God's created being), it will be much easier to give love to others. Most of you, like I used to, give out what you want. You help others so much because you need help. Reaping what you sow sounds right to plug here, but it doesn't match. You can only sow or plant when you have seeds. You only have seeds if you first had the fruit containing the seeds. If you do not return the seed of love to God who gave you the seed then you will never understand the concept of sowing what you have already reached. That is the way the universe works. God loves you, you love Him back, He gives so much love back to you that it overflows onto others because you want others to feel what you feel.

The best thing about self-love is that it only needs God and you. Everything else is a bonus. God created people for Himself and then other people for people. When you open yourself up to real love, you will see why loving yourself first is the best love.

Learning to Love What's Good for You

You can learn to love what's good for you. It's a process, and it is more than probable, it's very possible. People do it every day. In the 1990s most people didn't eat healthy and clean or go to the gym, but today it's very common.

Blaming love for remaining in a harmful relational situation is the culprit of not correctly directing the love that's in you. Think about what you're saying. God is love. So you're telling me that because you love someone, you're supposed to physically stay in an abusive situation? Stop blaming it on love. God loves everyone but He does not make excuses for individual disobedience. Agape is this kind of love. You can work to achieve, as close as you can get, the kind of love that God demonstrates. Agape love is unconditional, but it does not tolerate foolishness. It gently encourages right behavior, but it doesn't condone remaining in a harmful state of mind.

Love demands change. Remember, self-love is the best love. No one should use love as an excuse not to stay diligent in self-care. Staying in a situation where you are not appreciated but tolerated is unwise and it shows your weakness. It is not good for you. Whether you acknowledge it or not, people are watching you and waiting to see your next move. I'm not talking about haters waiting to see you fall. What about the people who care about you? Do you think it's right to give them the messed-up part of you? You direct your love in a place where you can never reciprocate from. No, you don't always gain from where you give, but a relationship carries more weight than if you're giving alms to strangers or those less fortunate than you. It's time to use love to strengthen you to change those areas that are not productive.

Waking up every day knowing there will be drama in your life that's causing you pain is not God's design. None of this is good for you. God cares about everything that concerns you (Psalms 138:8). This passage in the Bible says that God is working to perfect the things that concern you. Many understand incorrectly what it means for God to give you the desires of your heart. Sometimes your heart doesn't know what's best for you, but God does. If you are open to it, you will sense the desires God wants you to have. These are the things that you should go after. Many people have spent too many years on things that were detrimental to their lives. How did this happen? It is the result of going after your desires. God's plan is greater than anything you can imagine. The only drama that should be in your life is the excitement while anticipating the greatness that is next.

Love and hate are interchangeable in your willingness to do the work. You have to practice hating the things that God hates. Sometimes the things you should hate are attached to things you love so well. If you have a family member on drugs, you don't hate the relative, you hate the fact that they are on drugs. This is the same dynamic in relationships. You must admit you didn't always ask God what to do. You gathered up all of your intellect and natural prowess and went for your desires. Yes, you fell in love, but you put your love in the wrong place. It was never meant for you. You only knew the surface level of who you are, and you chose according to what you thought. It's time now to do the work of deciphering love and hate in a sensitive situation.

When you don't do the work to understand fully how to love and hate, you will never reach your full potential. I've heard the wealthiest place is the graveyard. That's because many never did the work I'm talking about now. People have spent their entire lives going after strong desires, putting all the energy in areas that never yielded proper results. You must learn to hate the things that may be good for someone else but not for you. God does not create a mess, but everything that is created is not for you to conquer. Believe me, do you have a truckload of wars that were designed for you to win? It is very frustrating to fight and fight and fight for something you can never have. You win some battles, but you lose three times as many. That's fighting the war. You are more than able to win the battles that were designed for you to win. It's okay to hate the things you're not designed to conquer, but it's not okay to add your love to it and fight a losing battle. These are battles you are not designed to win. Leave them for whom they were meant. Stay in your lane. It is so much easier to avoid what you hate. That is how God designed your life.

Once you acknowledge the things that bring you the most frustration, you will be able to see what you should hate. By no means am I telling you that life is easy. But you can tell the difference when God is helping you win. These are the things that are good for you. Learn to love them. Many are contained in what you learn, and the people you are around and in the mate, you choose to marry. Put your love here and hate the rest.

I have heard so many incidences about significant others struggling in the area of trust because of some maleficence in the relationship. Whatever happened is held over the head of the offender. Let me tell you something about me. I do not have to trust everything about you to love everything about you. What does that mean? You can love a person but not trust them 100%. I might trust them to cook for me but not trust them with my money. I wish I could stop all breakups that happen because of a little trust issue.

Trust is reckless because it is rare. You can't trust everyone in every area. You can't even trust yourself entirely. Put yourself in some compromising position, and you cannot guarantee that you won't... Whatever that is! People miss beautiful relationships because they do not know how to compartmentalize trust. When you are in a relationship, you must decide what you can and cannot live without. I have a secret you probably haven't heard: people are people everywhere. If you are human, you will mess up. Yes, even you. You cannot control trust. It pops up in areas in people's lives you may never expect. Trust it there!

I did not have my ex-wife's social security number, but she not only had my social security number but also all my personal information. I didn't even know she had three cellular numbers. I knew about and had only two of them. Maybe she wasn't hiding anything. It doesn't matter, but I must admit I felt a little something when that third number was revealed to me. Not sure why I was green in some of these areas, but when I learn, I adjust.

I'm better now because of what I've learned. One of the discomforts in my divorce was the fact that I expected others to treat me the way I treated them. That is too much trust. As I said, people are people. I have to admit I'm not perfect and neither is anybody else except Jesus. Trusting anyone wholeheartedly is wholeheartedly ignorant. Okay, you think you're supposed to? Psalms 118:8 says otherwise. What it says in essence is that it's better to trust God than think men will not fail you. Not only will other people let you down, on occasion you let yourself down. When all your trust is in God, He will never let you down. I learned this principle and can set my life up to protect myself from what I used to believe.

God is more interested in the protection of your heart than how you "feel" about other people. If you would be honest with yourself, you'll make adjustments in this area of trust so that you're less disappointed when things fall apart. You're not supposed to live like a cynic believing everyone is out to get you, but the wise thing to do is know where someone can be trusted. When someone shows you where they can be trusted, trust that. A person who throws caution to the wind will find their heart constantly in disrepair and the damage would be caused by them. Proverbs 4:23 instructs you to cover your heart because it holds all the issues of your life. You have to work hard at doing this. Once a heart is wounded it takes a while to heal. God knew this and put protective measures in place.

There are levels to my trust. It takes years to get to the top level. I might trust a person on one level, but another person may remain steady at the top level. This person has earned this position. This is not a strange setup. This is something couples must learn to do. Just because you love someone does not mean you open up every area of your life all at once. What if you love him, but he's a terrible money manager? Do you hand him the checkbook the day after you say "I do"? Why should you? He makes good money but is constantly finagling his way around his bills. You trust yourself in this area because you are never behind in paying bills and always have savings, investments, and money left in your spending account at the end of the month. He may be great in many other areas, but this is just not one. Leave him in the right level until he proves otherwise.

Years ago, one of my friends and I had a great discussion about the subject of trust. We discussed the following as an example of the various ways to trust people.

One friend, you can trust with all of your innermost secrets. You have confided and confided, felt better, and what you said has never come back to you from outside sources. His problem: he is constantly moving from one employer to the next. He would not make a good career adviser.

You can have another who is an excellent business partner, but you know he regularly cheats on his wife. You cannot leave him alone with your wife because you believe he will do what he does to most good-looking women—his best to get them in the bed.

Finally, you have a friend who is good to eat lunch with but is not very perceptive. He will give you advice that sets you up to be in pain. You can talk about the game last night, but problems you are having at work may be answered with a way to curse out your boss.

Each one of these people can be good friends, and they each have their place. You just cannot switch their locations in your psyche. You will mess up every time. If it's friend number one or two in the wrong trust level, you may have to restrain yourself from a physical altercation.

This may seem strange information in a book on marriage and other love relationships, but if you do not learn the art of placing trust, your relationship may be doomed before it can start. Displaced trust can mess you up for years. If you understand this in advance you can avoid some pitfalls. If you are already in and made the wrong decision about trust, that is okay too. Just stop and determine not to keep thinking the same thing will work next time. One wrong decision does not have to cancel out all the other right ones. Placing trust is a very important entity in a love relationship.

I learned some hard lessons by messing up badly. If you are anything like me, you want to listen to good advice when you do not know what to do. Find the areas where you can trust people, and you will surround yourself with wisdom you cannot pay for. Just like you, I can tell you what certain things won't work. Some ways are intrinsic in certain types of people. Once someone shows you who he is, believe him. When you learn lessons in the most difficult situations you become an expert in what not to do.

Put trust where it belongs and live your best life. Never attempt to make someone change his stripes. Every person has strong points as well as weak ones. Put the trust in the strong areas and reap the benefits. Unlike a zebra, a person can change his stripes, but he has to want to. Until that happens, trust where you know works.

The best lesson I have ever learned is how to love someone entirely without trusting everything about them. God loves us unconditionally, but He already knows He cannot trust us in every situation. That does not change His love. No, people are not God but can learn to love regardless of what is known. You want longevity in a relationship, practice this principle. This is a process I know will last my lifetime.

A Thin Line Between
Love and Hate

How can you hate someone whom you loved so desperately a few short years ago? I can tell you that. When you put your all into a relationship and your perception is that what you have put in has little to no reciprocal value, love can turn to hate over time. For a person who loves hard, it is easy to believe that if you put every ounce of your being, money, and time into your love life that you will create a consistent euphoric condition. You will learn that how you show love makes a difference in how you feel when a relationship fails. You are not the problem, but how you learned to love is.

I have mentioned it before and will most likely mention it again—you cannot change a person no matter how hard you try. My real issue was how could anyone allow someone to do all they know to make a relationship work knowing full well the feelings aren't mutual. It's not that complicated. You have to learn to love for the right reasons. If you are giving just to get from someone, you are doomed for much pain. You must love because it is the right thing to do. When there is no return, there is no return. You may be in a relationship where the other person has no intention of doing for you as you do for them. You cannot teach someone how to love you if they do not want to learn.

You can never put your expectations on another person who has not promised you anything. Expecting implies something is either probable or certain. After being with someone for any length of time you should know enough whether to expect certain things.

Time is a big factor. If after years you see no rewards for the work you're putting in, why are you still expecting?

You cannot be with someone for the rest of your life if you believe he should buy you a mansion in Cancun, but he's working as a team member at Mickey D's. Love is patient and kind and does not put demands on someone incapable of following through. After a while, you must believe what the person is saying in words and actions. Just because you believe something with all of your heart does not make it happen.

In 1996, actor Martin Lawrence starred in the film *Thin Line Between Love and Hate* with Lynn Whitfield. Martin Lawrence's character is a low-level womanizer with few finances, still living with his mother. Lynn Whitfield is a high-end woman who was lonely. She's been hurt in the past and is looking for a sincere relationship when she meets Martin Lawrence's character. The story does not go well because even though the lady expresses her expectations and what she won't tolerate, she receives exactly what she hates. He plays her by benefitting from her financial support yet still has other women, and in return almost loses his life at her hands. It's a comedy but has some harsh realities about unfulfilled expectations.

There is a thin line between love and hate. Your job is to know the line exists. Some things are easy to forgive while others are not. When you allow yourself to fall in love but cannot seem to get your target to love you as hard, love can turn into hate. When you begin to project that hate onto the object of your affection it only hurts you worst. It is a horrible cycle of torture. Do not allow yourself to cross the line from love to hate. How do you stop the forward progression? When you sense the change, take a step back. Did you give out of pride or real love? How long ago did you realize your man was not what you thought? When you answer these questions the truth will be your remedy. Most of the time you knew long before it got to this point. Most people do not change overnight. The truth was staring you in the face and you chose to complain and do nothing or completely ignore it. Let the line be your wall and stay on the loving side.

You can ask your significant other for everything you expect out of your relationship, but there's no guarantee all your dreams will come true. You cannot change a person, and there's no reason to go in expecting some things will come around. You must love yourself enough not to set yourself up for emotional abuse by lowering your expectations just to satisfy cheap ego or vain hopes. If the person isn't showing you hints of what you want from the start, you can just about guarantee that what you want will never manifest.

Many people have the character flaw of thinking that what they have to offer is so great they never have to change anything and they'll be accepted. This is the cause of the line being so thin between love and hate. Sometimes you can give your all and it will never be good enough. It hurts to know some people will never love or even like you just the way you are. The real problem is that they're not satisfied with themselves so they have no way of ever being satisfied with you. You can do two dozen backflips and an ungrateful person will look for more. The greatest freedom will be when you can accept some people just don't like you like that.

No matter how great you believe you are, you will never be 100% to everyone (most likely no one). A small adjustment here and there is fine, but a complete overhaul request is a sign you're not meeting your proper match. Get out as quickly as you can before you explode. You will never be enough for the person who just does not like you. Stop trying! If you take this advice you may never enter that hate zone. You'll arrive at that higher self-mode and realize you are good enough. Constructive criticism or self-evaluation is a positive tool. Make some adjustments because they can only help you. The other changes should be a matter of peaceful cohabitation. There is nothing you can do about how you feel about scrambled eggs. If you don't like them, you just don't. Being in a relationship is all about compromise. Everything isn't a deal-breaker. If you remain after uncovering more cons than pros, you are edging towards personal detriment. Stop trying if your efforts are not working. No one on this earth can make you be perfectly what he wants and vice versa.

You cannot be all things to everybody. Love you just like you are and upgrade the things that *you* desire. Do compromise, but some people will request a mile if you give them an inch. You can tell that when there are constant complaints about much of what you do. Maybe the complaints are unspoken, but *you* know. Instead of thinking someone will change, *you* change. The first change will be in your mind. Stop trying to please and just be the best you can be.

When you have done all you can to salvage a relationship and nothing is working, start making plans for the rest of your life. You owe it to yourself to maintain your sanity. Your emotional intelligence will tell you that you have done enough, and you gave it all you had. Staying and expecting different results will do nothing but make you blame the other person for all your woes. At this point, it's not the other person's fault. Take a close look at yourself and decide what you want. Get some counseling that may point out some principles you have violated in your own life that are causing you harm. The beginning of the rest of your life may take on the form of a sabbatical to make some life-changing decisions.

You can come out of hating someone. The first step is to forgive them for what you feel they did wrong in the relationship. This doesn't relieve them from any consequences they may have to suffer, but it does give you your much-needed peace. Stop revisiting all that went wrong while you were together. A relationship takes at least two people, and you're one of them. If a person showed you who they were and you didn't like it, but you stayed, whose fault is that? While you're forgiving them, forgive yourself for tolerating it too long. After forgiveness does its job, you will soon find the hating will end, and you may start seeing why you wanted the person in the first place. Let this happen. What sense is it to cross the line? Now the hate is subsiding.

When Your Heart Catches Up
with The Truth

L et's talk about when you've been through a bunch of crap and decide to stay anyway. Believe it or not, you go through the same up-and-down atmosphere whether you leave or stay. The only thing about staying is that some of the things that get on your nerves may never change but you decided not to leave; we're going to talk about that in this chapter.

So you decided to stay. You make all of these plans about the great new beginning you are to have with your spouse, and then the time starts ticking. Your emotions heard the plans, but your heart hasn't caught up. What about all you've been through? What about all you tolerated? She didn't say she was going to change. She just said she was sorry. Sometimes an apology has many nuances. You may be sorry you got caught. Yes, sorry you hurt me. But you have no intentions of changing. Remember—you decided to stay.

This was a very hard decision. You thought of all the years that have been put in, and you just don't want to think about letting them go to waste. Everything isn't bad; just some things. The decision has been made, and you're going to stay. That's a lot of weight on you. If you're going to stay, you can't bring up divorce every time you argue. Everything is not an irreconcilable difference. You are two different people striving to make some reconciliations and find some sameness. If what brought you to the verge of divorce is hurting you that bad, but you decided to stay, then maybe you need to talk to some other people. Get with someone with wisdom to help you go through the process of perceiving what you're dealing with in a new light. You decided to stay, remember?

There are consequences to every decision. You decided to stay, and now you're dealing with the backlash of your heart. At first, there may be disbelief of anything he/she says, and you're living in total distrust. You have to learn how to forgive because if you're going to stay unforgiveness in your heart will make your marriage a sham. You are guaranteed victory even if your spouse doesn't change. I'm not addressing an abusive situation. That's a different set of guidelines. Remember, you are responsible for your happiness. Unforgiveness will cause you more pain than whoever it is you're holding a grudge against. The consequence of your decision to stay in the healing of your heart while seeing every day the person who has caused emotional pain.

There's something funny about holding a grudge. If you never have to see a person who caused you pain, the grudge is not as active, at least physically. But living with someone who you're working on forgiving may cause you to act in a passive-aggressive manner. You can't do this either. You have to decide you will mature quickly in this area. It's called emotional intelligence. Grudges are for immature people. You may never have to stay in the company of someone who did you great harm, but you still must forgive them so you can heal. This does take work but can be done if you're willing. Decide you will not hold a grudge and then do the work to forgive.

Now that you've stayed, you have to decide you will not be a victim. There is a term used in psychology, and it's called "teaching people how to treat you." You do not have to do this in a physically aggressive manner. Now that you're staying with your spouse, you need to have some real talk about what you will and won't tolerate. You are talking to an adult just like yourself and cannot think you're going to dominate in this area while you are requesting proper treatment. You will tell them how it makes you feel when certain actions take place. If you both are willing to do the work it will take time, but it will be worth it. Remaining a victim never gets a person to the place where she wants to be. Unless you have some emotional dysfunction, you do not want to be patronized by your spouse. Both of you want equal footing and to be treated fairly. This can only be accomplished with mature talk. You are not a victim, and you will not make your spouse a victim with vengeance.

There will be some grief even though you stayed. You may question your decision. This too must pass. If you do the hard work of reconciliation, soon the pain will be in your distant past. There may be some times when you cry. This goes for men and women. No one wants to feel like they've been taken advantage of. But that's why there is a period of grief. Now, this may sound crazy, but did you know in the definition of grief is the word "distress"? You know nobody can live in distress every day of their life. If you've heard it before I'm going to tell you again—stress is not good for your heart. You must let the grief pass, and it will if you will allow it.

There's another unexpected emotion you probably never thought you would deal with, and that is hatred. As mentioned in the previous chapter there is a thin line between love and hate. How can you suddenly hate someone whom you once loved so dearly? Pain to a heart has a lot of twists and turns. Since you stayed, you will not hate the person for long. The real dislike comes from within you, and it's really aimed at yourself, but most people won't admit this and would rather turn it outward. What you hate is how you were treated. You don't hate the person. Hatred for a human being is hatred for life itself. You don't hate yourself, and you don't hate them. For the moment, your heart is lying to you. It's a protective mechanism. The Bible says to cover your heart because out of it comes the elements of your life (Proverbs 4:23). Your heart knows how to protect itself. If you allow the heart to do its work you will come through fine. For a God-fearing person, hatred is only a temporary dysfunction, because giving God your heart is what God requests. God created hate and knows better how to balance it in a yielded life.

When you come out of the roller-coaster of emotions and you are still staring your love interest in the face, you'll fall back in love. There is acceptance and quiet in this place. Now you're ready for another honeymoon. You may find yourself reacting in ways you thought were no longer in you. Go with it. You will find it was worth the trouble. Do some research, ask some couples who have been together for any length of time, and you'll see that any of them whoever decided to leave but didn't will give you the same course of events. The roller-coaster ride comes to an end. Nothing bad lasts forever. There's a season for good and a season for bed, but each one has its time limit.

Respect

There's one word that can conquer many things in life and weigh heavily in a marriage. It is the word "respect." To be clearer, I will say "mutual respect." Respect does not start with people. It starts with God and how you respect Him. If you make that where you start, mutual respect begins to take on a more important role in the union called marriage

When you use the respect of God as the foundational way that you live your life, many of your problems will disappear. When I was a teenager not only did I not respect God, but that neglect caused me not to respect myself or other people. The definition of respect includes giving someone or something high regard, esteem, or honor. One connotation of this word is respect as you see it in the Bible: "The fear of God is the beginning of wisdom" (Proverbs 9:10). But you have to be careful not to believe that respecting God is like the respect you give your boss so that he will give you a raise. God is not a man, and not respecting Him has more consequences than not respecting other authorities.

Respecting God is what gives you the substance of how to live a life that will make you happy and fulfilled. I believe the following passage puts this ideology in proper perspective:

"Fearing God is good because it saves us from caving into our sinful nature. That's why hearing someone is God-fearing makes us trust that person more. If they fear God, they are more likely to keep their word and treat others with kindness" (www.christianitytoday.com).

When you learn how to respect God, you will develop a love for Him that will automatically cause you to love and respect yourself and others, which includes your husband. This is a principle that can change your entire life. Respect will show you how to treat others in uncomfortable situations. Jesus demonstrated respect and shows you how to use it when things aren't going so well. One example of Jesus's respect for God is in the story of Jesus and His entourage. In that group was Peter. Near the time Jesus was going to be crucified, He and his boys ran into the authorities who wanted to arrest Him, but Peter wasn't having it. He was down with Jesus and at that time was the kind of partner you would want with you when the chips are down. As the enemies approached, Peter drew his sword and cut off the ear of the high priest's servant. What did Jesus do? He picked up the ear of the servant and put it back on the man's head. Jesus's respect for God stood up when it may have been better for Him to fight or run. He knew His purpose and trusted God to take care of Him (John 18). Jesus's love for God and His will caused Him to even bless His enemies.

Being a quick forgive is not an easy thing to do when you are not used to adhering to the concept of respect. Having mutual respect means that what you give out is what you receive. God set up the platform for giving and receiving. It is a universal principle that works. There is no need to attempt to manipulate an atmosphere that God controls. You do not have to demand respect. Respect returns on its own when it is incorporated into a relationship. When two people live in this arena, both will purposely desire to outdo each other in the love and respect that is shown. One of the greatest forms of respect is in the area of forgiving.

Many have a hard time forgiving because they believe they are opening themselves up for more pain if they do. Your fears only fuel your insecurities. When you react to a wrong based on insecurities, you only add fuel to the fire. Take a moment to think about why you feel the way you do and respond in accordance with what is real and not trumped up in your imagination. Some of your reactions are based on learned behavior. It started as your defense from real situations and it continued when you never fully dealt with the original cause of your discomfort. Your current relationship did not cause this dilemma and deserves a fresh start. Start doing the right things that may be at first uncomfortable. Forgiving is never the cause why you experience more pain.

If you learn how to respect God first you will begin respecting yourself and your reputation, because that's what you're damaging by your words, looks, and actions.

Respect covers more than just what you say, but also how you act. With the employment of respect, you may decide you do not want to marry this particular person. Maybe deal-breakers are present at the onset. Respect yourself and him by not going forward just to feed a lifetime fantasy. I've already decided I will give and expect a certain level of respect. I'm not marrying someone who shows me she will never agree with my drive. That is the epitome of unequally yoked. You can be unequally yoked and grow to be equally yoked, but this must be known in advance as part of the plan. If it's obvious this is not the case, you'll never get the respect you desire. This will destroy you. Talk about a thin line between love and hate. You will cross the line into hate very quickly. Then you will wonder why you decided to marry him/her. You can see his level of respect for what you represent if you are looking at more than just a good time on dates.

My respect for God not only fostered a love for myself but gave me a greater respect for those who God has allowed to enter my life for whatever reason. God knew exactly what He was doing when He gave you the knowledge to know how to put out what you want to receive. This act in and of itself builds my esteem and gives me the ability to look at others not as competitors, but as fellow citizens working to have a better life just like me. This sentiment is easily transferred to your significant other.

Decide to make changes in the area of respect and watch your life take on new meaning, making you know you have made the right decision in how you treat others. Respect this truth because it has the ability to ensure you reap what you put out. Your love relationships will take on a whole new meaning when you learn to respect the right of your husband not to agree with everything you do and think. This goes both ways. That is the reason the term is coined *mutual* respect.

A certain level of respect for the desires of your husband can assist you in expanding your bandwidth. It is a lesson in selflessness that results in elevation. What you do for him cannot be kept from you. Helping your man increase in stature by the level of respect you offer him raises the level of your stature. If you think you are honoring a king, then what does that make you?

Anger

nger is a natural emotion. The problem is that many do not research the reason for the anger, and they repeat it time and time again with the same results. It is not uncommon for things to bother you but getting to the root of your frustration will be a great lesson to learn. This chapter will deal with a subject I feel many never really understand. For a more productive life and better connections with people, it is good to know when you're angry, why are you angry, and how to channel that anger.

I have heard it said that men cry bullets. Now, I know every man does not get angry and instantly pick up a gun and shoot the source of the anger, but it is definitely a thought for many. Don't get me wrong, women get angry too, but it's acceptable in modern society for them also to cry. Pain is a real challenge for men. You most likely have heard it as a child—big boys don't cry. Whoever made that up should be nailed to the wall. Just kidding! But men should be taught how to channel their emotions when all they do most of the time is get angry.

Many relationship issues grow into the most hideous things because anger takes over in many situations that should be otherwise channeled. Ephesians 4:26 says it's okay to get angry but do not let the sun go down on your anger and do not allow anger to make you sin. What does this all mean? I have seen it for myself. A person may be angry about one thing, and that anger sprouts tentacles and reaches into other areas that have nothing to do with the original cause of the anger. The next thing you know, you can be ready to put yourself out of your misery by attacking the person who hurt you. The real culprit is unrequited anger. I believe the source of the anger comes from within. Yes, your spouse may have done something to make you upset, but instead of dealing with how you feel about what happened, you allowed yourself to take it down the road and turn simple anger into rage. I'm still studying why it's so hard to take responsibility for allowing some things to hurt you so badly. One reason is a character flaw that many people never deal with. It's called pride. No one is perfect. When people, especially men, learn it's okay to discover errors in judgment, I think anger can be solved much quicker. Relationships can continue into the future, or come to an expedited, peaceful end. Some relationships may even be able to continue if anger did not turn into sin and simple matters resolved with some truthful conversation.

When Jesus went into the temple and found people selling instead of praying, he turned over the tables and put those out who were not doing the right thing (Matthew 21:12). You have probably heard and know already that Jesus was without sin. His tumbling of the tables was an act of anger. You can get mad and slam a door, but it's when you start aiming cast iron skillets at someone's head that you've gone too far. A better scenario would have been to slam a door after you walk out of it and took a walk to cool off. Only return when you're ready to discuss the issue intelligently. Some subject matters are very close to your heart, and I understand that. You have to learn that acting out your anger does not solve your problem. Jesus turned over the tables, but He also solved the problem.

When you act out of sorts about a situation, the situation will remain if you do not deal with it correctly. Even loud yelling, threatening, and harsh stare-downs do not solve problems. Do you want your spouse to be afraid of you? If you answer yes to this, your problem is bigger than what I can write in this book. Maybe go to the gym and punch a few heavy bags. Do some amateur boxing. That's a place to let someone feel scared of you. Acts of rage in a relationship are harmful even if the relationship has ended or is ending. You both are still on the earth and are very much human. Talk to yourself, talk to a counselor, or pad yourself with some connections who have wisdom. This will help when your anger fogs your mind and you can't see an end to how you are thinking and feeling. Put your emotions in check and do not let anger be your guide.

Anger is good in its rightful place. It acts as a protector both physically and for your heart. It is a motivator to get some things done and is actually a healer. In its proper station in your life, it is a revealer of truth and lies. When anger is allowed to be in place too long it will screw up everything. It will spoil like milk. The container is still inviting, but the contents are distorted and good for nothing. Let anger do its job, and then replace it with the right emotion to continue living well.

"Being angry means we don't have to deal with why we are hurt, scared, or frustrated" (https://patch.com/michigan/grossepointe/dont-let-the-sun-go-down-on-your-anger). Do not allow this to be your stature in life. Become emotionally mature and deal with all of your feelings in a grown-up way. Because the truth is, many of the ways most people deal with their emotions are how they have dealt with them since they were children. Maturing means you deal with real, deep-down issues and come up better for it.

Don't suppress your anger but put it in the same box of toys that you place peace, joy, and happiness. It deserves a spot in your life, but never let it rule you. Although I dealt with masculine ways of anger, everyone can find themselves in this chapter. Stay in control of your emotions, use them wisely, never suppress them, but put them in their proper places when their time is up. Anger is the main one that can grow and sprout if not controlled. Suppression is never good but sprouting darts can be even worse.

Everyone Wants You Except the One You Are With

When a relationship is going south, your vision is 20/20 to all the others who are eyeing you. This is the most painful time in a relationship. This is when the place in your heart reserved for your spouse/lover begins to ache. "Why doesn't he love me like these others seem to? I see them looking. I hear and get the remarks." Maybe it's a mirage, or maybe "they" can see a heart that is breaking.

The grass is always greener on the other side, they say. At least, that's what you think when you are torn between staying or leaving your present situation. The truth is that sometimes the grass *is* greener on the other side. Where you are now may not be where you have to stay. You tell yourself that you do not want to get out for selfish reasons. You are trying to fix something that is irreparably damaged. Cars that are considered a total loss after an accident have had their main parts so badly damaged that the cost to replace them would be worth more than the car itself. It is only worth what a junk dealer can get for each undamaged part. Unfortunately, you are not a car. If you drag around a damaged heart it will damage everything you touch. The grass *is* sometimes greener on the other side.

There is one big problem with going to greener pastures—if you are not freshwater you can turn the grass brown. Repair work takes time. Those "others" are willing to wait if you are patiently working on yourself so that a new whole you travels to greener grass. There is nothing like leaving baggage behind, cleaning up, and presenting your suitors with an improved you ready for what is new. "They" may have wanted you from afar but will soon be disappointed if you do not get that heart fixed.

It is easy to believe the watchers want you. They may. The first line of attraction is what people see. They are looking at potential. They want what they see but do not always see what they're getting. Only you can reconcile your inside to what is presented on the outside.

Some relationships are redeemable, but others are functioning by routine. That means that all activity is performed with a joyless sense of order. When you are just going through the motions something has to give. If one or the other does not make a move, the relationship is already doomed. You both are living in a fake sense of decorum. Both parties must agree that changes have to be made. There is no hope for redemption without agreement. Robots have no heart and cannot make decisions. Relationships operating on what used to be are fair game for the "others" to hope them apart. If your relationship is redeemable then get it fixed; if it is dead then pull the plug.

Yes, "they" are eyeing you and have always been, but your happiness kept them at bay. The trip down south taken in your relationship has brought them close so that you now see "them" and they see you looking too. It's not new that they want you. Your vision for your relationship was once single, but now it is looking from side to side, hoping to be rescued. If you have been in your current relationship for some time it may be a little scary to think you can get back in the game. But don't start playing before you make a big decision. Do not let the others force you into a place you are not ready for.

Let them look, and you take your time. You know your relationship is over, but long-term relationships coming to an end don't always end quietly. You do not need the noise of other choices in your ear. There will be time for sweet whispers later on. Wait for the right time and start the next thing right. As long as the others have eyes they will still be looking.

Hope is Hurting Me

I always wondered why some people were stuck hoping for something to happen, yet the situation remained the same and the hope stayed deferred. I finally get it. You cannot put your hopes in things that involve someone else changing because there is no guarantee that this will ever happen. My wondering ended when I realized that some hope is placed on a fantasy that has no guarantee of ever happening.

Fantasy is a powerful thing. Webster's Dictionary describes it like this: "the power or process of creating especially unrealistic or improbable mental images in response to psychological need." *Wow*! That sums it up. I can tell you I found that fantasy often follows pain or trauma. To ease the pain in your brain, you conjure up an imaginary situation that will cause the pain to leave. This does not work. The reason is that if the fantasy involves another person, you have no control over their response to begging, pleading, or the condition of your mind. Fantasizing will mess you up if left unchecked.

Proverbs 13:12 (KJV) says, "Hope deferred (makes) the heart sick: but when the desire cometh, it is a tree of life." Now I completely understand how many people get heartsick. They have placed their hope in things that may or may not change. They may not realize how bad this is hurting them. Much time elapses and their hope still remains that their love will be returned the way they put it out. God does not even guarantee that. If you love right, you will be loved in return, but not necessarily from the person you poured your love into. To quench the drive of hope, you have to put your hope in things that are eternal and can never change.

One eternal guarantee is that you will get what you put out. If I think I can will someone else to love me, that is not eternal hope, that is fantasy. Remember the difference. Eternal hope will be answered but hope in what a person will do is fantasy. You must study what things give eternal guarantees.

The worst case of unrequited hope is when people are dating or even married to a person who has no intention or is unable to reciprocate what you are putting out. It would take a total remake from God to flip their heart. But in the meantime, your heart is crying out for comfort. Now I realize it is best to put your hope in something or someone who has a better chance at yielding good results, but if you are going to stay then you must redirect your expectations. Hope in this area is totally impossible especially if the person is incapable of giving back to you what you are giving to them.

The old church used to sing a song that says, "Build your hope in things eternal, hold to God's unchanging hand." God will never leave you hanging, but unfortunately, this is not the same with people. God knew this and made a way for you to escape severe pain. When you find yourself caught up in unbearable pain because someone you love does not love you back, there is an antidote. The culmination of all the biblical commandments is written in two statements. The second one gives you the instructions so you can heal. "And the second is like, namely this, Thou shalt love thy neighbor as thyself. There is none other commandment greater than these" (Mark 12:31). This is a commandment that will eternally make you free. No matter how much you love someone you cannot make them love you. Only God, being love Himself, will love you back like that because He loved you first, and that is eternal.

Do you know why good guys finish last? Because they do it all wrong. What they consider right has never been God's design. Everyone is created in a certain way. When they meet the one who fits, it is all good. Forcing someone to fit will never work. The authenticity of a person will be hiding in the shadows only to reveal him when you are all the way in. It was no magic trick; you just ignored the signs. You can ignite fantasy but for as long as you can, and he can suppress his real feelings for a little while. Make-believe is only cute for about two seconds. When life is real it can be painful. Putting yourself first is the only true practice of how to take care of someone else. You have to learn how to love other people the same way you love yourself. The word "good" in the first sentence in this paragraph is a substitute for ignorant. Learn how to finish first.

You are probably saying that you do love yourself. I'm sure you do, but it is the *way* that matters. You have to love people as you love yourself. If you rarely tell yourself "no" it will be extremely hard to hear no from someone else. Even a "no" to your advances will be difficult to receive. Maybe you never thought about it this way, but the practice to guard against pain starts with you. Love yourself enough to deny yourself things you believe you deserve. Saying no to you is one of the most powerful tools in self-love.

When a baby becomes a toddler, one of the first ways to make them upset is telling them not to do something or putting up a hand to stop them from doing something. From infancy to recognizing Mommy and Daddy, a baby is never told no. Even if they are, they have no concept of no. Some parents have never learned how to deny the baby, so the child grows up with a sense of entitlement. You may think this is a farfetched thought. Everyone is told no at some time, but it is the "no" that feels like rejection that is the most stinging to an adult. It started in childhood.

Not having your way is part of what you learn when coping with disappointment in both intellectual and emotional situations. Some of the greatest fights happen when a person refuses to give in when someone else does not agree. It is part of the maturing process. This is where you see adult bullies and those who use manipulation and retaliation in an attempt to get their way.

The reason why the above is the worst way to keep your hope alive is that you will keep getting the results you do not want. It is reciprocal. It will keep coming back again until you learn how to accept that someone is not going to cave under your pressure. As mentioned before, you have to put hope in its proper place. When an answer is "no" you must move on. No matter how bad you feel, it does not mean that someone will have a pity party with you.

One way to get over pain in this area is to give people the same space that you want, the right to feel like you want. Someone's rejection is another person's opportunity. It is such a time-waster to keep beating at a door that will not open. Get some counseling or go on a knocking hiatus. Do you want someone banging on your door when you don't feel like doing what they're asking?

The next lesson is a big one. A person may love you, but not like *that*. There are so many people in the world, you must take your time to choose your mate. Don't waste time having a childish tantrum because you want *that* but cannot seem to get that no matter how much you hope. The lesson is this—have patience with love because it will never fail. If you are giving out real love, it will come back just like that.

Never jump in head-first and expect everything will follow because you took action. You do not have that authority over your own life and definitely not over the life of someone else. Take rest in knowing that God desires to perfect everything that concerns you, even your love life (Psalms 138:8). Don't let hope fail you. Do all in your power that hope may be fulfilled, then wait patiently. Just because you press the elevator button ten times does not make the elevator come any quicker. But the elevator is going to come eventually. The same is true with life. Obsessing over what someone else refuses to do will not make them respond to you. Relax in hope and believe in the return of what you put out. And if you have released some things to other people that were not so good, you will not suffer for it forever. Forgive yourself and keep hope alive. Your well-thought-out actions are better than a cracked skull and a broken heart.

Hope is not supposed to hurt. When you take the right steps in life by trusting in the things that are guaranteed, hope will never fail! Hope in what you know will work and leave fantasy inside of fairytales. Hope is for daily use. The hope that hurts is not the kind that God wants you to live in.

If you want to Lose Weight, Get a Divorce!

For a couple of decades, I would hardly have said the words above. Yes, I had a few exceptions. As a pastor, I have had several opportunities to advise couples in trouble. Most of the stuff was workable. If both spouses would agree to make some changes together, there was hope that they could stay together. Then life hit me upside the head, and I knew that some marriages would have to end. Mine was one of them. I stayed married for twenty-two years doing what folks advised me to do. One thing I found out is that it takes two people fighting for the same thing for whatever it is to be won. I should have known these things with a divorce rate in America hovering around 50%. I would rather think that I and others could have been on the positive side of the 50% forever, but who am I to guarantee that to be reality? Sometimes marriage becomes an unwanted weight.

1 Corinthians 7:14-15, "For the unbelieving husband has been sanctified through his wife, and the unbelieving wife has been sanctified through her believing husband. Otherwise, your children would be unclean, but as it is, they are holy. But if the unbeliever leaves, let it be so. The brother or the sister is not bound in such circumstances; God has called us to live in peace." Go back and read that again. I want to explain something to you about this passage of scripture. It will tie into the first paragraph. Stick with me for a moment.

If you marry a person that does not have the same religious practices as you then you should understand that the "unbelieving" spouse is covered by your "believing". Even the children that do not seem to follow your practice are covered by your faith. All of that sounds good, but there is a catch and it can be found in the bible verse above. An unbeliever may just be the spouse that will never be agreeable, refuses to compromise, and is weighing you down because he has already left. Someone not believing in God may be easier to live with than someone who does not believe in you and what you stand for.

Some people that you and I know are staying with people who refuse to make any concessions. The marriage is there just for convenience, but they are suffering. Why do you hear so many people ask if someone is in a happy marriage? That is because some folks just learn to live with a spouse that is not trying to please them. No, the spouse does not physically leave, but they do not plan to change. Religious practice, like going to church every Sunday, means nothing if there is a train wreck at home. The opposing spouse will stay for as long as you tolerate their disdain for what you are requesting.

When I Googled how many people stay in unhappy relationships there were over three million hits. Many "experts" weighed in. Fifty years ago, two doctors coined the term "interdependence theory"; that was just the tip of the iceberg. Explanations went on and on. One study guesstimated that about 17% of people are in happy marriages! What? You mean to tell me that 83% of people that are married are suffering at home with a spouse that is not pleasing to them? I guess that is what that study is saying. With over three million internet subscribers weighing in on the subject, there has to be a huge portion of the population living miserably at home.

But, let me get back to the point of the unbelieving spouse leaving. Many do not leave. If all the amenities line up, why should he leave? The bills are paid, nice clothes are in the closet, two cars are in the garage and the kiddos are in private schools. What is so unhappy about that? Here is the problem: how you feel at home reaches beyond the front door of the house. You may stay and tolerate what does not seem to be changing, but that will not make your emotions and physical wellbeing any better. The spouse who refuses to make adjustments, also, does not have to be a traditional unbeliever. He may be a dogmatic believer in Jesus Christ. Maybe he comes to church every time the doors open. He can even be over the finance committee but, he refuses to give in to his wife's request. He may believe there is a God, but he is not going to adjust to other parts of the Bible that say to love your wife like Christ loves the church (Ephesians 5:25). This is the kind of unbelieving that mentally separates husbands and wives.

I believe that there may be some truths to the interdependence theory. This may not be the truth for all unhappy couples, but it may stand true for many of them. With both spouses working and keeping an appearance of peace to the public, why get out? If both are firm believers in the institution of marriage, then staying together may fall under the category of "must-do" no matter what. The interdependence theory is created on the premise of the first example that both are carrying some part of the marital load and it makes sense to stay for convenience.

Remember that the title of this book is Did God Tell You to Get Married. Since the name of God is being interjected then I want to deal with the other principles that need to be in place to keep a marriage together. Staying together should not be drudgery. No one should be glad to work late just so that they do not have to come home. Hanging out with friends should not be more exciting than cuddling in the bedroom. There is a balance to everything, but the developments of habits used to escape home are a sure sign that something is wrong. God does not usually come down and introduce people to each other, but choosing the correct mate does have a lot to do with who you are and what you want.

I am not sure how the numbers became so skewed for unhappy marriages, but I do believe that this can change if people look further into whom they marry and get out when it is over. Just because someone does not physically leave does not mean that they have not already left. I think that most unhappy marriages are not marriages, but roommate privileges and non-friends with some benefits. I guess the divorce rate would be higher if some of these "fake" marriages ended.

Losing the weight of a bad marriage has a cost. It is not easy and it is not cheap. It plays on your psyche and disturbs your "normal" life pattern. Unless a spouse is lying in the bed twenty-four seven and only getting up to bathe and eat, you will know that they are no longer there if you call it quits. But, because of what I said earlier about the unbelieving spouse not leaving, on occasion somebody HAS to make a decision.

Unbelieving in the above scripture is talking about the husband or wife who does not believe in Christ, but there is more to believing in Christ than saying you do. Marriage is a job. If God does not sustain it, it is doomed from the start. Before I end this chapter on losing the weight of a spouse, I must say that God may not tell you who to marry, but He can put people together who want to stay together. The desire, from both spouses, to stay together brings the sacrifice of compromising. If one compromises and the other does not there is a problem. When God puts people together based on their desire to marry then both will work on following the principles that God designed to keep them together.

Marriage takes two. There should be some pre-marital discussions about expectations. When Tina Turner sang "What's Love Got to Do with It?" some believing folks did not like those words. The truth is that it takes more than eros (sexual) love to keep a marriage together although this part is also very important. Both spouses must want to keep the other spouse happy and sometimes that happy pendulum swings way to the left for a little while. If patience is employed, the happy will swing the other way very quickly.

When both spouses are working to make the other a priority, what can break that up?

You may have gotten married at twenty-one, but at thirty-five you are more mature. Both of you should be maturing together. Just as you are more experienced in the workforce, you are becoming more experienced at home. You both have learned each other and the nuances are speaking for themselves. It is when one person is ignoring the requests (spoken or unspoken) that there is a storm brewing. Never take it for granted because your spouse is not screaming and yelling for change that he or she is okay with the status quo. You are smarter than when you first got married and you know when things are not the same. I have heard so many spouses say that they were surprised when the divorce papers came in the mail. If you are paying attention to your spouse, it should not be a surprise. You are no longer a child and nobody is going to tell you how to fix some things unless you are asking. Keep a check-up going and make some adjustments. Twenty-one years old is no longer your excuse.

Only you know when the weight is too much to bear. You may have tried, made your own adjustments, or begged for change. Just because he is not leaving does not mean that he has not left. Just because she is not complaining does not mean that she is not waiting for you to make a move. No one is designed to carry the weight of an unhappy marriage. It shows whether you think you are hiding it or not. I am not confirming whether someone should get a divorce or not. It is a personal decision because you have to live with that. But, I do know that marriage is not meant to be a weight-bearing institution.

Becoming one in spirit is the goal and that can only be done when two people agree that that is the direction. Just like in the natural, losing weight is no easy task, neither is the weight loss of a divorce. But, for the maintenance of peace of mind, it is sometimes necessary. The becoming one never materialized and it was just a matter of time.

Have you ever seen someone post-divorce and she seems so free and contented? The marriage was a weight. I have never read anywhere "the burden of being married". I can only recommend that you do everything there is to stay married, but both of you must want to. If your spouse will not go to counseling, you go. If he refuses to make any changes for you, you know what's up. Everything in scripture is not always literal. Keep waiting for that husband whose heart is way across town to pack his bags and leave. That may never happen. In the meantime, you are burdened with the weight of a non-marriage. God did not put you together and you cannot keep it together no matter how hard you try. When enough strength is gathered to end this cohabitation, you will know that you are now free.

The weight you lose is spiritual, intellectual, and emotional. There has been a spiritual battle waged against you. You wonder why you cannot seem to pray right, eat right and not get enough sleep. You are living with someone who needs help to move out. Your intelligence is being insulted. You know that he does not want you and he is lying when asked. You suppress the truth for the sake of appearances, children, or pride. Appearances can be deceiving; the children will start acting out if not checked and God cannot assist you if you live inside of your pride. It may be hard, but getting close enough to God can relieve the struggle of hard decisions.

Running to Prosperity

P rosperity is a mindset. It is the freedom to live in your own authenticity. When you are in a love relationship it is very easy to lose touch with a part of who you are. When you stay together that suppressed you may not need to surface. It is not a deal-breaker. If the relationship comes to an end it may be an opportunity to find those places that bring prosperity to that single you. You and he may have always gone on vacation together because that is what he wanted. Your prosperity in this area comes from your alone time. Prosperity is personal. It is a mindset that brings you personal opulence.

My relationship lasted over twenty years. There were many reasons why it lasted so long. Most of the reasons were not my own, they came from well-intentioned people who I allowed to form my value and worth. Pouring the honesty of what I was feeling yielded the same results. This was not prosperous for me. The longevity did not make a difference in the content of what I experienced.

I was not allowing prosperity to invade my life. As I stayed, I felt like I was living a lie because I was. The general public had no idea. There was no authenticity to what I was presenting. Prosperity only manifests in people who are being honest with God and themselves.

Whether you have been married for one year or twenty, divorce is a painful thing. For those who experience no pain, there may be some underlying reason that I have not yet discovered. Unless you married for other than love, you do not go in with the expectations of getting out soon. Most of you probably did not consider getting out at all. I know some say that they will try it out to see if it will work. For these people, they leave themselves an out and that leaves wiggle room from the beginning, but, living with someone for any length of time under the covering of marriage, is not an easy thing to dismiss after being committed.

Like any other decision in life, divorce takes a toll on your emotions. It does not matter which of you filed for divorce. Ending a relationship with someone you wanted to be with is not easy. While in the middle of the proceedings you will go through a myriad of emotions, but there is a better at the end. You cannot see it while you are in it, but keep moving and you will get to a place of peace in your emotions.

One of the first keys to getting through the consequence of divorce is to allow you to mourn. This person was part of your life. You did things together. You planned things together. Hell, he/she was the beneficiary of your life insurance policy. Now, s/he is dead to you. Whether you had kids or not he was part of your world. Now that part is no more. Your children still have their daddy, but you are no longer his wife. That stings, even if the divorce was your idea. Let yourself feel the pain. It is easier to grieve today than be bitter for the rest of your life.

Grief will not be the only emotion that you deal with. Face the truth that you were not perfect in the marriage. You will be hit with the reality of your character flaws. It does not matter how many you come face-to-face with, you must stare them down and work on each one. Even if you have decided that you will never marry again (most likely not true) you want to build relationships that do not have to feel with your rough edges. On the real tip, you want to make yourself better for your next go-round. No matter how many feelings come up, put them in compartments and work through each of them.

Out of all the emotions that make up who you are guilt is a big one. You must first forgive yourself. If you do not do that, you will take yourself with you just the way you are. That may not be a pretty picture. If you do not change and learn to like yourself, you will take bitter you into the next relationship. Take time out to be alone and find out who you are now and reconnect with the good parts of what you used to be. Your forgiveness may be the fact that you feel stupid for staying in a bad relationship for so long or you may regret the activities that brought your marriage to an abrupt end. Whatever the circumstances, you must work through them by first forgiving yourself and liking the authentic you.

Who were you before you got married? Maybe that person got lost in the life of your relationship. What were your dreams and aspirations? Did you put yourself to the side while working to please your person? If so, you are still here and have time to recoup what you feel you lost. As long as you are above ground there is always a chance to find that person you lost some time ago.

While you are finding yourself again you may discover some part of you that you did not know that you had. Maybe it will be the ability to say, "No" or to take you to the movies. Maybe you did not know that you like to work out, now going to the gym is part of your routine. Sometimes marriage will hide from you what was always inside of you. This did not have to be the case, but it just happened to you and some others.

On the road running to prosperity, you will finally bump into an activity called dating. I am surprised to find that so many people never understood the art of dating. Every relationship was entered with the hopes of ending in marriage. That ain't fun. That goes back to the title of this book. Not only did God not tell you to get married, but you also did not even give yourself permission. You just got married. This will not happen if you stop and have some fun while dating. I'm not talking about jumping in and out of the bed. I'm suggesting you add some variety to your life, by loosening up. Go out for coffee, to the movies, have a quiet meal at a small bistro or invite him over for a meal then tell him to go home. Nothing's wrong with that. If you want to remarry someday then give yourself time to enjoy being single. An unhappy single can lead to a miserable married person. The word prosperity does not fit in the life of someone looking for someone else to fulfill them.

The last mile in your road to prosperity is learning to manage your life without the perks of having a person. Whether the two of you got along or not you were a couple. Now some of the things that your person did are in your hands. That's okay. You will find that you are better than you thought. You can handle all the finances even if you did not before. Being a good manager is in everyone. Some folks just had the privilege of having others that handled some things for them. After divorce, that may be over. There is a whole world out there waiting for you to enter, run to it.

When you have done the work and your mind has settled into your new reality, you will be ready for the prosperity that has awaited you. I have seen some that never evolve and remain in a place as a victim. These kinds of people just complain about what used to be. They cannot believe that their life has changed so dramatically. Their grief stays so long that the blame game becomes part of their daily thought life. Don't you be like that! Everyone gets a chance to prosper and what better time than after a painful divorce. It is over. Walkthrough your steps of change and then run straight to your prosperous place.

- Prosperity is a mindset.
- Prosperity is personal.
- Prosperity only manifests in people who are being honest with God and themselves.
- Prosperity does not fit in the life of someone looking for someone else to fulfill them.
- When you have done the work and your mind has settled into your new reality, you will be ready for prosperity.

Things to Remember

After reading the ups and downs of a divorce and the victories that can be found in marriage you decided that whether God told you to get married or not you are going to make it work. I commend you. There are some good marriages out there that just need a tune-up. I discussed many things in this book. In this chapter, I want to revisit the principles as a way of giving you one place to do some referencing. This book should serve as one of your many references to securing your lifelong relationship with your spouse.

1. When I talked about cutting the cord, I realized that this may prove hard for some of you to do. You have to remember that the point is not to cut yourself off permanently from your birth family, but to establish the roots of your own family. You will build new traditions and renew the familiar ones. It will be a fresh start together with your spouse. This new unit will set its own standards. When you rejoin the family where you were raised you will merge the old with the new and add extensions to the family tree. It is an ever-developing family that existed for many previous generations and will continue. Yours is a part but deserves its own heritage.

2. Although you are now part of a new branch you may have carried some old habits with you that did not benefit the home where you grew up and are causing problems now. These issues must be dissected and discarded. This is not a simple task, but the proper application of principles can be changed. No family functions at 100%, all families have

their dysfunctions. You have to be aware of your generational bad habits and decide that you will do all you can to not continue them in your new family. This has to be a decision on your part because like the home where you were raised, these behaviors may be deal-breakers.

3. One habit that you may have brought along is complaining about but not doing anything about the way you look. You have control over your own body. You can choose to make your body style the "it thing". Be the best you that you can be. Your attitude is what will make the difference in how you are received. Any way you slice it you must take on the mindset that how you look does matter.

4. On the other hand, you also have the power to do something about your looks. Do not wait till your husband leaves you because you have let yourself go then go running to the gym talking about, "I'm getting my sexy back!" What's wrong with staying sexy in this relationship? If he still leaves after you have done all that you can for him, then you are already in the game. You then just stay in the gym and do not have to up your time to two a day. The main thing is to not let you go. Why does someone have to tell you when you can see it for yourself?

5. Never let it be said that you use sex as a bargaining tool in your marriage. Sex is what will bring you together and keep the lines of communication open in your relationship. You will never have to be jealous of what someone else has to offer if you keep it spicy in your bedroom. Sex can be a peacemaker. When you know that your sex life is thriving it makes all other areas seem minimal. Just keep in mind that sex cannot pay bills or break deal-breaker habits. But it is not a negotiating tool and should never be used to blackmail your spouse. This kind of tactic most likely will backfire on you!

6. I touched on a very important topic of raising stepchildren. While working on this book I was given a valuable lesson on this subject. I know now that children play a very important role in how "step" parenting plays out. The parents should know the rules and adhere to form a successful bond between parent and "adopted" child. The word step is not necessarily derogative and can be the source of a loving connection as long as a parent knows that he is marrying the mother and her child or children and vice versa.

7. Finally, on the topic of the Family Anointing, the example of family principles was laid out for you. You were able to see that Adam walked with God in perfect harmony. This is a picture of what should happen in a family with a sure foundation. The man should pray and ask God for guidance and God should be the center and the source of all that goes on. Noah had a global vision for his family. His vision not only saved his family but preserved the life of all living things on earth. Your vision should be expanded to ensure that all that your family does can reach the next generation. Abraham's faith not only is an example for you today but gave him the right to be called God's friend and put him in right standing with God despite his character flaws.

8. The last example is one that stands the test of time but will take you into eternity. Jesus Christ is the epitome of a perfect human being and an obedient son. He had no wife because the entire church is His bride. He showed you how to live under the strain of adversities, love your enemies and live in harmony with your family, friends, and neighbors.

9. There is nothing here that if applied will bring you grief. Take them and use them. Add your flavor and watch the metamorphosis. You do not have to wait until your spouse changes his habits for you to change yours. You want to work on yourself because it is the right thing to do. Even if you know that God did not tell you to get married or you

doubt whether God ever tells anyone ever to get married most marriages have a thousand reasons to be saved. Yours is no different.

10. Your marriage does not have to be in trouble for you to decide to add to your "divorce-proof" weapons. You do not have to do it for your spouse, do it for yourself. Things you do for yourself tend to be more successful. Your joy will come from within and whatever your spouse adds will be an embellishment.

I desire that you have an excellent future and a displayable marriage that is just as good behind closed doors like the one you show in public.

Prayer

God, I ask that you bless each person who reads this book. I pray that every decision they make will be theirs alone because whatever they decide and whomever they decide to be with, the decision is theirs. He or she, not anyone else, has to live with his or her decision. I pray for you to bless them with peace. I pray for peace for their past and for any experience or decision they've made up until this date. May they have peace with what has already been done. I pray for peace for their present and I pray for peace for their future. Whatever situation they are in today may they seek Your guidance and follow Your will for them. No matter what situation they are in, I pray they understand that all things work together for good and that You will allow everything to work out for their good. They've gained experience from their past, no decision they've made was in vain. I pray that they've experienced the love needed to be fulfilled and happy for the rest of their life. No one can give anyone the happiness they need; each individual is responsible for and can guarantee happiness only for himself or herself. I pray that You, God, will give them peace for their experience and for the experience of love to be fulfilled in their life.

About the Author

A nthony Murray is The Unlocker. He is a trendsetter, visionary, transformational speaker, and innovative entrepreneur. His genius is extracting what is special about people and finding the message they've been hiding, the expertise they've downplayed, or the skills they haven't been able to bring to the forefront. He helps people uncover their true strengths so they can leverage them for whatever it is that they want, whether that is a better job, starting a business, getting a promotion, or simply the satisfaction of doing something amazing.

Anthony Murray has an innovative vision and the gift to see what God is doing next. With a fresh and relevant voice, Anthony Murray relates to all genres of people, from the wealthy to the poor, blue-collar or white-collar, street hustlers, drug dealers, ballplayers, millennials to baby boomers, and spiritual leaders. His goal is always to find common ground and help people at their place of need.

For over 15 years Anthony Murray has led Oasis Family Life Church a ministry that he founded now serving in 2 locations in the Atlanta area. Through his real-life practical teaching, he engages multicultural and multigenerational audiences from various social and religious backgrounds. This down-to-earth approach is just one of the reasons he's built long-lasting relationships with entertainers, professional athletes, politicians, entrepreneurs, and other ministers of the gospel.

A highly sought out speaker, mentor, and advisor, Anthony Murray inspires people to dream and do the necessary work to fulfill their dream. Through his coaching programs, he teaches others how to increase profitability and marketability by solving problems.

He travels the world igniting people to dream again with his bestselling book What Happened to your Dreams. He delivers the word of God with humor and practical knowledge which enables people to apply it to their everyday lives

www.ingramcontent.com/pod-product-compliance
Lightning Source LLC
Chambersburg PA
CBHW070444090426
42735CB00012B/2459